In the Name of God, Most Gracious, Most Merciful

GUIDING LOVE BOOK II

(My Graceful Father & The Wolf)

Safieh Laaly

ISBN: 978-1-917636-51-3 (Ebook)
ISBN: 978-1-7320565-1-0 (Paperback)
ISBN: 978-1-917636-52-0 (Hardcover)

To my Dearest Grandchildren

In gratitude for unveiling a new dimension of love
that surpassed my wildest imagination.

I once thought I had poured all my love and strength
into cherishing my children, but you showed me that
there is always room to love more.

An Account of a Forgotten Human Passion

in the World of Matter

For the young and the young at heart

Table of Contents

With Gratitude

To my family, friends, and beyond, who have
inspired me in this journey.

The pleasure of knowing each and every one of you is
a constant reminder of the countless blessings in this
fascinating world.

Many had tried to extinguish his divine breath, but it was ordained in the protected tablets of Truth that he must rule and establish justice for all.

With "Love," he must face the dangers alone, liberate the world from calamities, conquer the uphill battle of widespread corruption, and deliver his adversaries, including his own brothers, from the depth of darkness into the Light.

Behzawd

My Graceful Father

Chapter 1 The Journey

All day long, I, Behzawd, tried to distract my youngest son, Nimaw, from missing his brother, Pawkzawd. We were lost without him as we had never been apart before.

Praying in my heart, I could barely conceal my agonizing anxiety for his sake. We took aimless, restless walks toward the path we expected him to appear from any moment as we played around with no focus or joy.

Having faith helped me stay composed and keep calm. I knew it would all be the way God intended it to be. Relying on experience and patience, I accepted that everything was exactly the way it must be. As difficult as it was, I needed a deeper understanding to unlock the mysteries of what was before me. That was God's promise, and whose promise was more reliable than his.

I was four or five years old when I first discovered that there was an answer to every question that arose in my mind before I even thought about it. With a sense of curiosity, I intentionally stretched the time between the suggestive answer in my thoughts and my subsequent actions. Regardless of how long I paused,

I felt assured that the answers came from a trustworthy, all-knowing inner voice that was always present.

Curiously, I found that leaping ahead of this inner voice led to undesirable outcomes, prompting me to delve deeper and recognize the authenticity of its guidance. A conscious twist of intention often proved detrimental to achieving favorable results. I learned to take an active role in manifesting this inner voice by truly listening to my intuitive thoughts. This experience required a conscious effort to discern the purity of my intentions, and to set aside my own intellectual reasoning in order to receive the guidance that was being revealed to my heart.

With time, it became as simple as recognizing my intuition and using my judgment to attune myself to a higher purpose of existence. When I learned to recognize and resist the allure of immediate gratification, despite the challenges it posed, I began to savor the sweetness of more rewarding outcomes, even if they felt distant and elusive.

Enduring the pain of recognizing when and where I had dismissed the warning signs of my inner voice brought about a constant sense of remorse, urging me to stay alert. This awareness led me to consider my options more than twice, with a renewed focus on seeking the divine presence in my daily life.

The time I needed to sort the confusing elements out was critical, as I learned to embrace patience as a virtue. Like ascending a staircase, my conscience took the lead towards a deeper understanding.

In dealing with my brother, Howmi, there was a persisting threat of descension that could send me back to a new start every time. With patience and practice, however, new layers of wisdom slowly shed light on how to steer clear of the next conflict.

Like a matrix of light expanding from the depth of my existence, the rays bent with flexibility in every struggle. In the process, it strengthened my faith by seeking harmony according to the divine order. It was a constant evaluation of the divinity of the challenge as I watched the dichotomy of the outer world in contrast with my inner world.

Contemplating the sibling rivalry that is as old as human civilization kept me fearful of the outcome of when one brother envied the other and said:

"I will kill you!"

But the other, who was anchored by faith, saw beyond his immediate circumstances,

"God only accepts the offering of the sincerely devout. If you raise your hand to kill me, I will not raise mine to kill you because I fear God, the Lord of all worlds. I want to let you bear your sin against me along with your other sins; then you will be one of those destined to burn, and that is the reward of the wrongdoers."

Alas, in their case, the whisperer convinced the first in his rage to kill his own brother. Then, he became lost and was filled with regrets.

The aftermath of that sibling rivalry continues to this day. Their childish envy has torn families apart for ages, which, in the best of scenarios, has left deep scars and broken hearts to endure for generations to come.

As harmless as the shallow ripples of siblings' rivalry may seem at the moment, given the time and momentum, they can turn into a tsunami that destroys everything in its path. Nevertheless, this destructive human behavior is widely accepted today as a "natural" human behavior.

Our current journey meanders through the tangled webs of sibling rivalry that were woven through history by imperfect human behavior, not being grateful to a Perfect Creator.

Chapter 2 Great Grand Parents

L ike his fathers, Farshawd, the favorite noble son of Farsaw, was from a lineage of truthful men, highly revered in his village and beyond.

Farshawd's wife, Pari, daughter of Zia, had inherited her character traits from her divine ancestry that were traced back to the honorable survivor of The Great Flood. Her modesty concealed her inner strength. With God at the core of her humble teachings, her faith was manifested in patience, hope, and caring for others.

The town's people talked a lot about her grace;

"In my days, Pari shines like the sun. Even in my darkest moments, her kind words light up my spirit."

"The Light of Pari's kindness outshines the sun in the sky of my life."

"Listening to Pari cures my pain, and new hopes come to light for me just like the stars that show up from nowhere at twilight. Her words help me articulate my thoughts…"

But Pari and Farshawd were troubled by a deep heartache despite everything they had going for them in the world.

Concerned about the long-term impact of emotional friction between their twin sons, Farshawd and Pari sensed they needed some kind of intervention. Their exhausting efforts were fruitless. Any hope of seeing their adolescent sons grow out of their differences with maturity was diminishing as they watched them drift apart.

Farshawd always found ways to cheer up everyone, especially his hard-working, beautiful wife. His hopeful thoughts and unique sense of humor lightened the burden on her distressed shoulders for a few moments at a time.

"My dearest one, Pari, it is just a matter of time. Howmi will soon understand that he is the one missing the most; he will learn to join in the fun, be patient, just a little longer. You will see soon."

To appreciate his efforts and kind words, she smiled every time ever since the twins were little toddlers, but at thirteen, it was hard to convince anyone that things would change for the better any time soon.

The mesmerizing summer night chorus of crickets and frogs under the full moon had cradled most to deep sleep. Pari's eyes were wide open, troubled by her motherly worries.

"What is going through my sons' heads right now? How could we help them love one another? Could their troubled hearts ever heal by their brotherly love?"

She turned and tossed in bed.

Farshawd put his gentle hand on her shoulder "Are you okay, my love?" quickly wiped off her tears before turning to her side to face him.

"Yeh"

"Let me see."

he looked closer

"No, what is troubling you?"

"Nothing, dear, go back to sleep."

"I cannot sleep when you are like this."

"Sorry, my love, just worried. Your health is in danger. Our sons are suffering, Bahzawd is exhausted from trying, and our family is in distress."

"shush… common"

softly put his pointing finger on her lips

"Sweetheart, I am fine. Everything will be alright."

Her tears shimmered in the moonlight flowing

down her cheeks. The long, skinny shadows from the veranda's columns divided the room into uneven, tilted rectangles. A gentle breeze blew in with the sweet air of honeysuckles' fragrance from the garden below.

With one hand, he ran his fingers through her hair to brush it away from her face, and with the other, he wiped off her tears.

"Don't worry, my love, they are growing up. Soon, they will grow out of their differences and become best friends; you will see."

But she was restless and agitated beyond wishful thinking.

"We are not sure when that would happen, if ever."

Deep in his heart, he knew she was right. He paused, then took a deep breath.

"What would you suggest, my love? Do you have something in mind?"

quickly, she sat up, energized with excitement

"Yes, I do. Indeed I do, I have been thinking… umm… what if Behzawd went to live with my brother for a while?"

Silence…

He was thoughtfully caressing her hand with his pointing finger.

"That would be a huge imposition on Sir Kia."

her excitement elevated

"It might be a great help for Kia, too, while giving our sons a chance to miss each other."

He always valued her well-grounded opinion.

"You may be right, my dear; if they missed each other, they may recognize their love for one another."

She took his hands and kissed his palms repeatedly with excitement from a new hope.

"Behzawd will be just the right help for Kia, like a son he never had. Oh, Kia will be so happy."

Farshawd opened his arms to invite her back to sleep. She rested her head on his chest. With his arms wrapped around her, they cuddled, trying to go back to sleep. But she could not shut her eyes close, staring into a bitter-sweet life without Behzawd around.

Chapter 3 The Annual Event

The afternoon heat was subsiding. The jovial people of Mihan were putting the final touches on a huge cake. Angelic voices sang special songs, reminding the festive evening for a special occasion. The air was filled with the heavenly aroma of a Thanksgiving meal that was prepared for thousands, mixed with the fragrance of the flowers.

The people in Mihan, from farmers and craftsmen to chefs, cleaners, and distributors, showed their loyalty and gratitude in their own ways towards my parents, Pari and Farshawd. They were revered as blessings from heaven for their leadership and selfless services.

It was not a coincidence that the city's biggest annal event was on my birthday. With it approaching, I was more hopeful for a new chance to get close to my twin brother, Howmi. It was now a bigger deal because we were turning thirteen, known for its "becoming of age."

Men were considered grownups at thirteen. Howmi was much bigger and stronger in body than me. I yearned to make him happy and have fun with him. Regardless of our differences, I was determined to

11

make that birthday special for my brother.

I spotted him by the pond and walked over to him. On my way, I picked up two bowls of fruit mix from the table at the food stance.

"Howmi, would you like some of this delicious fruit bowl?"

He ignored my stretched hand holding the fruit bowl. I bent over, put the bowl on the ground next to him, and sat down a couple of feet away to give him space.

"It is all yours, ummm… very fresh! How does it taste to you?"

I put another spoonful in my mouth.

"Ah, it tastes great, here, try it. Would you care to go for a swim after this?"

"No, I am tired."

Then, he stayed quiet. I knew better than to push the issue.

"Hey, Behzawd"

Someone yelled to get my attention.

"Come on, let's go for a swim."

I did not want to leave Howmi

"Have fun, I might join you later."

People were socializing around the self-served snacks and refreshments stands.

A gentle breeze whispered through the drooping willow branches nearby. The melody of the little waterfall pouring into the pond below was soothing.

"This is great, isn't it bro?"

Suddenly, I felt a shiver going through my spine, and then, a feeling of sorrow fell upon me. It had happened before. I knew something unpleasant was about to happen.

My seven-year-old sister, Farah, was sitting with a couple of her friends just a few feet from us. Her long-braided hair was tied with a red bow and tucked behind her back. They were happy playing with their feet in the water. Farah began to sing a song for the fish that she made up as her friends laughed following the end of her song:

"You are beautiful, free to swim, little fish, big fish, red and white fish, swim my little fish, swim my big fish, swim my red fish, swim my white fish…" her sweet voice turned into a giggle:

"Oh, the big fish wants to eat my foot."

They giggled together

"Come and look, Behzawd, Howmi, come here, look, he is hungry."

Like always, she was on her mission to feed the creatures within sight because they were hungry. I rushed over with my fruit bowl. She moved to open a space for me. I gave her the fruit bowl as I sat by her side. Farah dropped the fruits one by one. We watched the fish snatch and tear them into pieces to swallow until the bowl was empty. She had saved the fish from hunger, happily and content.

Farah was energetic, full of life, thoughtful, kind, and she always went out of her way to make her other brother, Howmi, who did not want to have much to do with anything, happy.

Howmi could see everything from the same spot I had just left him. It was his favorite seat-rock. He looked the other way if anyone looked at him. Showing no interest in getting involved.

Farah noticed a butterfly on the ground struggling to fly with its helpless wings flapping. She put the empty bowl down and rushed to the rescue. Her friends followed. I watched her adorable facial expressions.

"Aw, poor little beauty."

The girls were traumatized. Farah's pronounced lips and creased forehead sympathized with every move the little creature made. She gently picked up the half-living butterfly and placed it in the palm of her hand.

"You are still so beautiful. Don't you want to fly?"

Farah had to protect the little creature from the girls who wanted to touch it. She was very careful not to let the air blow it away as she walked over and held it in front of Howmi.

"Look, Howmi, what should we do? This poor butterfly can't fly, isn't she beautiful?"

To her surprise, Howmi pushed her hand away, stumped his feet on the ground, and paced across the garden and up the stairs.

In shock, Farah tried to be strong. She could not let anyone see her tears as she bent over, picked up the slow-flapping butterfly, walked over as she talked with it, and gently rested it on a bright yellow sunflower in the nearest garden.

"I hope this makes you feel better and get strong; try to fly; you must be scared."

Then, she discretely wiped off her tears and walked back to her friends, who had forgotten about the butterfly since Farah had gone to show it to Howmi.

"Hey, look at that big white fish; it likes to bite; that one has a big tommy! "one of the girls chimed in

"It ate too much. "they giggled, splashing water with their feet into the air towards the fish.

Farah was walking back with a smile to hide her sorrow, still recovering. I stayed where she had left me in case she needed support.

Our parents were surrounded by people under and around the shade of the big central gazebo. Although from that distance, they could not hear what was said, they saw everything. Father was listening to mother's answer to someone from the crowd. I remembered the hopeful comments she had repeated in our conversations.

"Howmi is sensitive, and he expresses his emotions differently than most. He was different since he was born; be patient, he will grow out of it soon ..."

I did not understand the meaning of soon anymore. The emotional toll on my father's health and my little sister made me anxious.

Chapter 4 The Town

Mihan was a small town where everyone knew each other, and people tended to their daily affairs without worry. It was built on natural terrain with minimal physical barriers between the communal housing. All the living necessities were cultivated, manufactured, and distributed locally throughout the year.

At the skirts of the mountain, multiple springs bubbled out of the aged rocks and joined further down to form the Baraka River. Rich with aquatic life, the reiver was like the soul of the town that cultivated not only the agricultural lands but also the livelihood of the people. As the town's main recreational corridor, its shores embodied memories and stories in its constant flow.

The town's hub was a vast central open space surrounded by buildings that fitted in and followed the topography of the land. Monumental gateways separated the hub from its outer ring. Building facades were delicately designed with exquisite details. Manmade masterpieces were sculpted out of rocks and met natural elements with dramatic effects.

Families' private living quarters were separated by

architectural partitions. Each building was flanked with roofed verandas on both sides, overlooking its inner-side gardens, ponds, and the town's activities and events. The shops surrounded the buildings beyond their outer-side orchards, farms, and pastures.

Men worked in the shops and farmed the lands on the outer side and joined their families for breaks and at the end of the day. Women managed domestic affairs in the inner spaces as they nurtured, supervised, and educated the young.

Throughout the year, the hub attracted people of all ages to play, celebrate, dance, participate in activities, and even mourn together. Activities were organized for each age group by its seniors and managed by experienced leaders. Meals were prepared in the open and served to everyone, including the occasional wayfarers.

Large, raised platforms were surrounded by colorful landscaped gardens of flowers, herbs, and specimen trees. Each platform could accommodate group activities for hundreds of people at a time in major events. The palm-leaf roofed gazebos around the ponds were a popular refuge from the hot sun. Natural stone benches and tables were tucked under the large trees to make more shaded spaces for smaller gatherings.

The highest level of the flat lands contained a fishpond, and its perimeter was lined with stepping-stones that were partially submerged in the water. The half-submerged rocks were the perfect seat for younger children to sit on and play while watching and learning about aquatic life.

With the cascading land, ponds grew in size and depth. In the lowest level, the pond looked more like a small lake. This was a major recreational hub that attracted youth and families for swimming and canoeing.

A small branch of the Baraka River carried crystal clear water to all residences as it meandered through the hub with mesmerizing effects. Its alignment was perfectly designed to irrigate the gardens. It created a small waterfall pouring into the ponds, which had dramatic effects as it cascaded down the slopes.

The hub's irrigation system was engineered throughout its gardens. A network of six to eight-foot-wide berms separated the gardens and served multiple purposes. Kids loved to use the berms as racetracks. Their challenge was to stay atop while running.

Chapter 5 Family Puzzle

As the sun set, the pink clouds shimmered with a silvery glow. The town's annual celebration buzzed with joyful singing, playful melodies, and delicious feasting.

Howmi had spent most of the afternoon on the veranda. It was his birthday, and I hoped he would join in the festivities. I observed him from a distance as he descended the steps and made his way to a tree. He reached up to pluck a fruit from its branches. Above all else, I longed to be his friend, especially now that we were officially considered grownups at thirteen. I ran towards him:

"Hey, Howmi! Those mouthwatering apricots you just picked look delicious. Let's pick some more for others. Would you help me?"

He ignored me, but my desire to reach out to him was greater than I could give up. Hoping to make a positive impression, I continued with my exciting one-way conversation:

"I can climb up high to pick the best ones for you to catch."

Suddenly, he shouted:

"Get away from me."

I paused for a moment, feeling a bit hesitant, but I knew I had to show him my sincerity. Determined and eager to prove myself, I rolled up the sleeves of my robe and tucked it into my pants. As I reached out to grab the sturdy trunk of the tree to climb up, he suddenly shouted once more:

"I can do it by myself."

To my surprise, he decided to pick the fruit in his own unique way. He forcefully tugged at a branch that was already slightly bent from the weight of the abundant apricots. In an instant, the branch snapped right before our eyes. Despite the unforeseen mishap, Howmi remained unfazed. He calmly selected one ripe apricot, took a satisfying bite, and then turned around, making his way back up the stairs with a carefree stride.

I stood there, feeling a mix of emotions and a heavy heart as I watched the broken tree. It felt as if my hopes of getting closer to my brother were slowly fading away. A lump formed in my throat, making it painful to swallow. With a voice filled with anguish, I could only whisper my pain out into the heavens.

"Oh, Lord! Only You Can make peace between our hearts. I love my brother. Help me hold him in my arms. Teach me how to show my love."

I surveyed the scene. Father was talking with a group of people in a distance, and a little further, Mother was engrossed in a lively discussion with a cluster of ladies. I decided to join her and settled myself near her. Her face, adorned with a delicate white shawl, exuded kindness. Her long, flowing blue ensemble gracefully reached down to her ankles, making her appear even more angelic than usual.

She graciously excused herself from the group of ladies and made her way towards me. Taking a seat by my side, she gently placed her hand on my shoulder. Just her touch was a world of love and comfort. Overwhelmed with love and gratitude, I held her other hand in mine, showering it with kisses. Her soft fingers tenderly lifted my chin, and as I met her gaze, I felt a surge of strength and reassurance.

"Oh, dearest mother! It happened again. I'm at a loss for what to do. Every moment of laughter seems to effortlessly turn into tears. Just look at father, how burdened with sadness he appears. I believe he witnessed everything. It fills my heart with fear for his well-being. Mother, please know that I love you, and I hold love for everyone in my heart. I long for a way to transform this world of unhappiness. How can I bring about positive change?"

Tears gleamed in her eyes, shimmering with overflowing compassion.

"I am immensely proud of you, my sweet son,"

she whispered tenderly.

"I know it's incredibly challenging for you to endure this burden. However, I simply cannot bear the thought of losing either one of you."

She paused momentarily, her voice catching in her throat as she struggled to compose herself. Her grip on my hands tightened, seeking solace and support.

"My dear son, you hold such significance in Howmi's life. He loves you deeply, even if he struggles to express it at times. Can you find it in your heart to be patient for a little while longer? Perhaps he will overcome his internal struggles sooner than we anticipate. Let us look ahead to the joyous years that await us, filled with hope and happiness."

"But mother, you know that may never happen into his adulthood unless something is done about it. You have hoped for 13 years! I wonder if he would feel better if I did not exist!"

She wrapped her arms around me, holding me tight.

"I mean, Howmi would probably feel better if he did not see me around."

Her warm embrace conveyed a deep sense of love and reassurance.

"You are a source of love and support for him, even if it's not always easy for him to show it. Your presence in his life is meaningful, and while it may take time for him to understand and express his feelings, it does not mean that he would feel better without you around."

With a tremor in her voice, she expressed her concern, her words laced with fear and worry.

"My sweetheart, the mere thought of being apart from you deeply saddens me. Howmi holds a deep affection for you, even if it may not always be evident. Let us have a heartfelt discussion with your father about this, but we must approach it with gentleness and consideration for his health condition. Your happiness is paramount to us, and we will do everything we can to find a resolution that brings joy and harmony to our family."

The earnest desire to bring peace to my parents weighed heavily on my heart, and my mother understood its significance. Just as we were discussing possible solutions, a lady approached my mother, seeking her attention. Before leaving to assist her, my mother planted a tender kiss on my cheek and squeezed my hands tightly, reassuring me of her immediate return.

A few yards away, Farah's butterfly continued to flutter its wings in a delicate and unhurried manner. It seemed like its final moments were near. I could not help but be reminded of my father's condition.

I swiftly wiped away my tears when I caught sight of mother's returning.

She sat by my side, and we watched the little girls playing by the pond. Gently, with a hint of urgency, I spoke up to pick up an important conversation:

"Mother, the sight of that butterfly's fleeting moments reminds me of how precious time is. We need to find a way to address the father's condition. It weighs heavily on my heart, and I know it does on yours, too. I think Howmi would feel better if I were not around, don't you think? I must go away."

As if sensing the weight of our conversation, Farah swiftly broke free from her group of friends and raced towards us. Her footsteps left little wet marks behind her, reflecting her hurried pace. She went around us and wrapped both of her arms around my neck from behind, squeezing tightly. Her embrace brought a comforting warmth that eased the turmoil in my heart.

"Where do you want to go, Behzawd? Can I go with you?"

"My dear Farah, you have very sharp ears!"

Just as I began to turn and face her, Farah tenderly embraced my head in her arms tightly, drawing me close to her chest. As she gently released her hold, I took her hands into mine and met her gaze with gratitude and sincerity.

"There are some things I need to discover and sort out myself, taking you with me in my heart."

Our eyes locked, a silent understanding passed between us that spoke volumes of the bond we shared.

"But I don't know where I am going sis! Plus, who would care for mom and dad here?"

A soft smile graced Farah's face, radiating a deep sense of satisfaction and determination. It was as if she had accepted the responsibility that lay ahead with unwavering willingness.

Her grip on my hands tightened with a sense of longing and uncertainty. A future she could not quite comprehend. I reassured her with a comforting smile, silently promising that we would face whatever challenges lay ahead, hand in hand.

Chapter 6 A Glimpse of Hope

The full moon was coming up to illuminate an already captivating night sky. Mother and I strolled together, heading home after attending a charity event. Farah had departed earlier with father since he was not feeling well. Howmi had opted to remain home, choosing solitude over joining in the evening's festivities.

Each moment spent in the company of my mother felt incredibly precious. As we walked beneath the expanse of the night sky, we couldn't help but marvel at the sight of the majestic moon and the guiding stars. There was a sense of solace and wonder in their presence. We silently shared a profound appreciation for the inherent beauty of the universe surrounding us.

In that enchanting moment, mother abruptly halted our walk, directing her gaze towards me. Her hands tenderly rested upon my shoulders, emanating warmth and reassurance.

"My dear son, I want you to know that I have not stopped thinking about what you said. You are the fruit of my love, and I want nothing more than to help you be happy and succeed."

I listened intently, my heart filled with gratitude

and love as her sincere words echoed in my ears and pierced through my pains.

"I know, mother. Don't worry. Everything will be alright. Your unwavering support means the world to me."

"God Willing, everything will be alright, my love. You deserve to be happy. I am not sure how I can bear life without you around, but I was wondering if you would be interested in living with your Uncle Kia for a while."

A sudden mix of emotions washed over me. The thought caught me off guard.

"Are you alright, mother? Really? Do you mean it?"

I saw the shimmering tears in her eyes under the soft glow of the moonlight as she nodded in agreement. Her willingness to sacrifice her own happiness for mine overwhelmed me with a mix of gratitude and sadness. The unbearable lump in my throat held back a whirlwind of emotions. We surrendered to the depth of our bond as we embraced with sighs and sobs.

Her palms alternated between covering my face and accepting my soft kisses upon them. I was overwhelmed with love and appreciation that words could not express.

Thoughts of the possibilities ahead filled my mind, intertwined with a mixture of fear and hope. But despite the overwhelming uncertainty, hope shone bright in the darkness of the unknown. The moon and stars silently witnessed. I gently held her hands on my shoulders.

"Oh, mother! I would love to see him. I remember him from when I was little. How old was I, mother?"

"Humm… If I recall correctly, you were around four when he visited us with his whole family."

"I remember being very happy."

I gently wrapped one arm around her shoulders as we continued our walk.

I stopped and looked into my mother's eyes.

"I remember when he read us a book with magical characters. I loved playing with his children. They were two, right mother?"

"Yes, my sweetheart. Remember his two daughters?"

"Oh, yes, and Uncle was so kind. He was everyone's father. Remember the stories you told us about growing up with him? They made me imagine what the special bond and love between siblings could be like. I wish my love had the same power to heal and mend my relationship with Howmi."

"My dear child, I know how long you have waited for a close bond with Howmi. Be patient. Perhaps he will miss you by being apart for a little while, which may help him realize his love for you."

"That would be my dream come true, mother."

"Hold on to that dream, my son; it will come true one day and will guide you through your journey."

"I will be missing my brother and everyone here. But I will do my best to help Uncle Kia and enjoy his kind presence. Even thinking about him brings happiness to my world."

Our walk home transformed into a graceful dance under the enchanting moonlight. I twirled around mother, capturing her in my arms, savoring every tender moment. The world around us faded into the background, leaving only the ethereal connection we shared. I kissed her hands with frequent turns as we continued down the path.

"I am positive you will be a great help to Uncle Kia. You know, you will be the son he never had."

"Oh, yes, mother. I would do anything to help

him."

Not only was the possibility of living with Uncle Kia exciting, but it also felt like opening a sunny window to a new world that I had been dreaming of for a long time.

A thousand thoughts raced through my mind. What would happen to my dear family if I wasn't around? Could it be that my not being here might actually help reduce the stress that the doctor said was causing my father's extreme fatigue and sudden weight loss? What we did know for sure was that father could use a calm and tranquil atmosphere to heal. His energy was drained from constantly witnessing his sons' quarrels.

The only thing to do within my power was to distance myself from the constant clashes with Howami. If I could just stay out of his sight, it would be a big step towards calming him down.

On the other hand, the city of Sawmawn, province of Marz, where Uncle Kia lived, was far away. If I go, it might be a while before I can return.

"What if something happened to father? I might never see him again!"

Chapter 7 The Paradox

S hould I choose to stay and be there for my father as his health declines, supporting him through this challenging time while fueling his pain from watching Howmi's occasional tantrums, just as everyone else does? Or should I gather the strength to bear the pain of separation and venture onto a new path?

Howmi's outbursts were often physical and aggressive towards me, which caused a lot of harm. It made me wonder if I stayed away. Maybe he wouldn't get so irritated. That would be a much more peaceful and less stressful atmosphere for our father.

What if his anger is directed at someone else in my absence? Who could that be?

The thought was troubling, but there was no other choice. I had to find a way to avoid him. It was impossible to know when his anger would flare up again. Despite my best efforts, his fights would inevitably keep coming.

I tried to imagine embarking on a journey into the unknown. It made me nervous. But what scared me more was the constant tension of walking on eggshells. Despite everyone's best intentions, Howmi always found ways to argue and vent his anger.

The idea of being apart from my beloved family filled me with unease, making my tummy churn. Yet, deep down, I knew it wasn't the end of the world. I realized that I had the ability to make a positive impact and lessen the worries by easing some of the tension. Maybe I was preparing myself for the emotional challenges ahead. As the days passed, I pondered upon the possibilities that awaited me in the next phase of my life.

I had always been with my family, never apart from them. Could my absence bring positive changes to our family dynamics? And my father's health? Could it improve or worsen my father's health? If I managed to survive the wilderness, I might find a way back to visit them soon in the future. Uncle Kia could certainly use a helping hand."

Chapter 8 The Last Straw

Early in the morning, I was about to leave for the fields as usual. On my best days, Grandpa Farsaw joined me and nourished my soul with his wisdom and love. On the way out, I caressed the dew off the glistening weeping leaves of a Copper Beech tree. I was using my robe to wipe my hands dry when I spotted Howmi strolling by the pond with Canaan, our friendly sheep dog.

What a lovely day it would be if it began with befriending my brother.

"O dear, my Lord, I place my trust in You. Please Bless us with grace."

The second I stepped down the stairs, Canaan ran towards me.

"Good morning, brother."

Canaan reached me overjoyed. His tail wagged rapidly. He couldn't contain his excitement, leaping and spinning around me, his fluffy backside sticking up in the air. His adorable face expressed how excited he was to come along with me on whatever adventure awaited.

I gently patted Canaan on the head, trying to soothe him and encourage patience as I continued facing Howmi.

"What a lovely day! Would you like to join me in exploring the fields?"

But, in a burst of excitement, Howmi yelled:

"No, you cannot take him with you."

As I gazed at the worried dog, my heart filled with compassion. I had to act swiftly to diffuse the tension before things escalated.

I knelt down and gently directed Canaan to return to Howmi.

"Oh, sure. Are you going somewhere with him?"

Howmi seemed satisfied with my response and didn't say anything, but the dog was anxious to leave with me.

"Hey, body, run along with Howmi."

I padded Canaan on its hind, encouraging him to make his way towards Howmi.

"Maybe tomorrow, fellow, common body, run, run along."

padding him to cooperate, but he did not respond.

"Howmi is waiting for you, common, I have to go. I'll see you soon."

I began walking towards the gate. But Canaan had made up his mind to keep me company and barked with excitement. Howmi was coming towards us with obvious anger that riled the dog even more.

I sat on the ground to calm down Canaan. His posture was pleading to go. I caressed his face, acknowledging his enthusiasm.

"Buddy, I cannot take you today, common. Go with Howmi."

Howmi caught up and pushed me to the ground, separating me from the dog. Surprised by the force of the push, I fell back on the ground. Howmi swiftly grabbed hold of the barking dog's ears, firmly pulling him with clear commands.

"Be quiet, I said quiet, run."

The dog's barking escalated into a frantic commotion. I couldn't help but worry about the potential disruption it could cause to our sleeping parents.

I had to end this encounter before things turned

uglier. Without uttering a word, I got up and ran up the stairs to my room. The dog managed to free himself from Howmi's grip and darted after me. He halted at the foot of the stairs, anticipating my return.

As Howmi forcibly pulled Canaan away, I heard the sorrowful cry from my furry friend. Feeling disoriented and unsure of what was happening, I hastily gathered a few essential items and packed them into my travel bag. With one final glance around, I slung the bag around my neck and shoulder and made my way out, compelled to leave in a rush.

With uncertainty, I paused at the bottom of the stairs. I couldn't bear to depart without bidding farewell to my mother and my father one last time. The thought tugged at my heart, making it difficult to proceed.

With a heavy heart, I looked up towards the doorway of their room. My beautiful mother was standing there, like a statue, frozen in a mixture of sadness and hope. My torn emotions tugged me in different directions.

"She must have watched the whole thing."

I whispered to myself.

"So sorry mother. My sweet mother. Please forgive

me. I love you."

My heavy heart felt lodged in my throat, making it difficult to breathe. I must slip away before we both reach our breaking point. The least I could do was to spare her the additional burden of my anguish.

"Please forgive me, dear mother. I must go now, or I won't have the strength to leave."

With a soft whisper and gentle wave of one hand, I tapped against my chest with my other hand to show her special place in my heart. Then, with a mix of reluctance and uncertainty, I turned around and began to walk away.

I could still hear Canaan's barks echoing from a distance. As I reached the gate, I looked back to see mother one last time. Placing my hand on my heart, I offered her a final farewell with a respectful bow.

In her most heartwarming gesture, she had both hands on her heart, then crossed her arms for a virtual hug. Overwhelmed with emotions, I swiftly exited through the gate, venturing into the sprawling fields to the northeast.

"Oh, gracious Lord, I humbly seek Your will in this moment of uncertainty. Humbly, I ask for Your wisdom and guidance to lead me along this path.

Please grant me the strength and clarity I need to navigate through the challenges ahead."

My tears began to flow freely now that I was out of her sight.

"Dear Lord, I believe that this is the only way within my power to bring peace to my family. I humbly ask for Your guidance and confirmation that I am on the right path. Please light the way and show me the steps I should take."

To my right, the sun was rising on the horizon, casting a long shadow that seemed to tug me back toward where I had come from. With great effort, I pushed my weary body to keep moving forward as my trembling legs could give way at any moment. I longed to steal another glance at her, but various obstacles obstructed my view, denying me the chance.

My thoughts were clouded by sorrow, fear, and doubt, creating a dense fog of uncertainty. I had to redirect my focus toward the potential for a positive outcome that awaited me beyond this painful experience.

"My beloved mother and father, please do not fret for my well-being. I assure you that, in due time, I will return as our Lord Deems fit. May peace be upon us; peace be upon all."

Chapter 9 Into the Unknown

The morning air felt suffocating as I grappled with the guilt of leaving without bidding a proper farewell. The quarrel over Canaan seemed trivial, yet I knew that any other disagreement had the potential to escalate to a far more disastrous outcome. It would have taken an uglier turn if I had not withdrawn to spare everyone from further pain.

As tears streamed down my face, I remained resolute in my choice not to give in to the temptation of going back home despite my father's illness. The weight of uncertainty lingered in my heart. I realized that I may never have the chance to see him alive again.

I walked for hours in a northward direction, my heart heavy with sorrow and my emotions in turmoil. Lost in my thoughts, I allowed my subconscious to guide my steps, paying little attention to the world around me. As the sun started to set over the majestic mountains to my left, a newfound sense of purpose slowly emerged within me, unveiling the true reason for my journey.

I relied solely on the sky and the knowledge of a city called Sawmawn, located to the north in the province of Mihan. The extent of my journey was uncertain. I had never ventured such a long distance before, especially on my own and on foot.

I was exhausted. The heat of the day gradually subsided with the setting sun. From the fear of giving in to regret and turning back, I had been tirelessly walking, almost running, throughout the day. Now, enveloped by the majestic mountains, under the starry sky, and accompanied by the sounds of the wilderness, I finally allowed myself to pause. "I can stop running now," I whispered to myself.

I surrendered myself to the serenity of the moment, fully immersed in the tranquility that surrounded me. Opening my senses, I listened intently to the symphony of the natural world. I embraced each sound as it intertwined with the stillness of the night.

In my hurried departure, I managed to take a few precious loaves of bread that my mother had baked, a small water bottle crafted by my dear grandpa Farsaw from goat skin, and a set of clothes for the journey ahead. These items became my sole source of nourishment and a powerful reminder of the love and care that my family had bestowed upon me.

I quenched my thirst with a sip of water, realizing that I had gone the entire day without eating or drinking. This was not hard since I had grown accustomed to fasting most days while working in the fields. This resilience and familiarity with fasting helped me push forward, drawing strength from past experiences to endure the challenges that lay ahead.

As I continued to walk, I realized I had to take care of myself and prevent my body from growing weak. With this in mind, I scanned the surroundings for a safe place to rest for the night. To my delight, I spotted a rocky flat top situated on higher ground. I climbed up to the spot. It was spacious enough for me to stretch out comfortably. I took off my shoes. My feet were swollen and covered in blisters from the straps. With a sigh of relief, I whispered, "Ah, this is better."

To attend to my rumbling stomach, I took a bite from one of the pieces of bread, savoring its simple nourishment. The flavors filled my mouth. I couldn't help but be grateful to my Lord as I whispered.

"This is delicious. Thank you, Lord."

I stripped off my long robe, repurposed it as a covering, and created a makeshift pillow with my stuffed bag. Then, I eased myself down and allowed my weary body to rest flat on the ground.

Since departing from the fields, I had not encountered another soul along my path. The realization of this solitude struck me deeply.

"What a long and peculiar day it has been," I muttered to myself, feeling a mix of weariness and curiosity. I wondered how long it would be before I reached another semblance of civilization, longing for the warmth of human interaction once again.

I decided to set that thought aside for the time being since it only heightened my worries. Looking at the starlit sky, a profound sense of tranquility enveloped me. All worries about the past and future faded away. I was able to fully embrace the present and took a deep breath, "Ah! This is beautiful."

The surrounding tree canopy stood tall and sparse, allowing glimpses of the stars that began to twinkle in the sky one by one. I noticed their sparkling beauty in a profound sense of awe. A deep appreciation welled up within me. "This is a truly wonderful world," I whispered softly, cherishing the enchanting sight before me.

As I marveled at the magnificence of the world around me, a profound sensation washed over me — I was not alone. In the midst of this vast and wondrous creation, I sensed a connection to something great. The beauty before me echoed a divine presence, reminding me that I was a part of something much greater existence. Overwhelmed with gratitude, I whispered, "Thank you, Lord."

My soul was enveloped with a delightful rush of warmth, instilling within me a newfound sense of freedom and liberation that I had never experienced before.

In awe of the vastness and intricacy of the havens, I acknowledged the immense power and knowledge of the One who created them. The full moon steadily ascended higher in the sky, illuminating the night with its glow. I wondered about the harmonious order of the universe with each star in its orbit. The blinking stars, like tiny beacons of inspiration, beckoned me to contemplate the complex infinity of galaxies that lay beyond our reach. I was filled with reverence as I whispered words of adoration and admiration for the Lord.

"You are Magnificent, Lord. You have created this marvelous universe with a purpose."

The understanding dawned upon me so clearly that there exists a deep connection between every aspect of the world and its Creator. Therefore, as a small particle within the grand design, I, too, held a vital place in the intricate tapestry of existence. Although the vastness of the divine plan surpassed my limited understanding, I was humbled to recognize my place and purpose within it. I felt an unwavering sense of connection to the divine world, knowing that I was an integral part of something much greater than myself.

I was struck by the incredible power and vast knowledge possessed by the One who had brought everything into existence. It became evident to me that such an awe-inspiring creation was not without purpose. The divine intention behind it all unfolds according to His Wisdom and Purpose. He Is Mighty Powerful and all-encompassing in Knowledge.

The full moon ascended higher in the sky, casting a gentle glow on the world below. I marveled at the infinite universe in that deep blue starry night. I wondered about the meaning of the blinking stars and contemplated the boundless galaxies that lay beyond.

I found myself overwhelmed by the sheer grandeur of it all and could not help whispering with awe, "You are Magnificent, Lord."

Divine beauty was manifested in every celestial spectacle before me.

During the many nights I had spent in the open fields with my beloved grandfather, he had taught me a great deal about the stars as he imparted knowledge of the significance of their locations, the patterns of constellations, and their practical use in navigating the Earth's terrains.

I realized the importance of preparing a celestial map to guide me along the way on my journey to the north of my hometown of Mihan. My celestial knowledge was a powerful tool and comforting connection to the night skies that I would use as my compass and guide on this demanding voyage.

Chapter 10 Heavenly Map

I have always been enchanted by the stars at night. My grandpa and parents were my wise teachers as they guided me to learn and appreciate the wonders of nature. On my especially precious nights, even after a long day of work, I would venture back to the open fields, sometimes with grandpa by my side. There, we would find ourselves utterly captivated, basking in the awe-inspiring beauty of the vastness of the heavens as we spent hours studying the stars in wonder.

Grandpa's words were etched in my heart.

"The North Star, Polaris, is the best compass to find our way around at night."

Knowing so little about how to reach Uncle Kia's house, I only had one clue - his house was situated beyond the mountains, in the northern direction of Mihan, where I had left my parents behind. With this in mind, I knew that following the steadfast path of Polaris, the North Star, would lead me straight to my destination.

As I watched the stars emerge in the northern sky, a celestial map began to form in my mind. I identified the seven stars of the Little Dipper, also known as Ursa

Minor or the Little Bear. Just above the Little Dipper, I spotted the two distinctive upside-down pointer stars, Dubhe and Merak, residing in the bowl of the Big Dipper. With this celestial guide etched in my memory, I extended an imaginary line from Dubhe to Merak, leading straight to Polaris, the North Star. Now equipped with this celestial map, I felt fully prepared to navigate my way toward Uncle Kia's City of Sawman.

I carefully reviewed my mental map several times, double-checking for any possible errors.

To stay on track, I must follow the extended end of the Little Dipper handle, ensuring that I keep heading in the northerly direction. In doing so consistently, I knew that Polaris would steadily ascend higher in the sky relative to my position with each passing night.

I felt a profound connection with the universe, a revelation that filled me with awe and wonder. It was a realization that had eluded me in my ignorance before. Fully immersed in contemplation, I surrendered myself to a tranquil slumber as the soothing embrace of the night carried me away.

Chapter 11 In the Wilderness

I was awakened by the whimsical melody of a bird. Was it dawn? Disoriented, I glanced around at the surreal scenery that enveloped a deep sense of peace and tranquility. To my left, a peek-a-boo moon emitted a soft, radiant glow against the majestic backdrop of the deep blue starry sky. Memories of the previous day flooded my mind. I felt revitalized and ready to embrace the day ahead. A part of me longed to forge forward with determination, yet another part struggled with past hurts and wished to find solace in retreat.

Suddenly, a gentle breeze wrapped around me like a comforting embrace that gently persuaded me to let go of the painful memories and focus on the present moment.

As the daylight burst through the darkness, a melodious chorus of chirping embraced the air. The enchanting melody of nature's wild symphony resonated with the joyful awakening of the early birds eager to partake in the celebration of yet another magnificent day.

My feet throbbed, swollen and ablaze with discomfort. As I tried to tie the straps of my shoes, the pressure only aggravated the blisters beneath. Reluctantly, I stowed my shoes in my bag and began walking barefoot, hoping to evade the risk of infection should they burst open.

Gazing up at my guide—the vast sky—I checked my bearings against my mental celestial map. With a deep breath, I summoned my determination and set forth on my journey, each step infused with steadfast resolve and unwavering commitment.

I walked nonstop until dusk. The first few days, I walked through the days and rested during the nights. But the scorching heat of midday became overwhelming, urging me to modify my schedule. I opted to rest during the hottest hours and resumed walking when the moon illuminated the night, which added a dash of adventure to my journey.

Once I could wear my shoes again, I accelerated my pace and extended my hours of travel. Each morning greeted me with a breathtaking display of colors as the sun gracefully emerged on the horizon, painting the sky with a touch of surreal beauty.

As the moon progressed to thin crescents at its cycle's edges, the nighttime illumination grew dim, making navigation more challenging. Plus, traveling during the night came with its own set of difficulties and dangers. I had to be cautious and take calculated steps to stay on the right path. I was well aware that a fall on the rocks or plants or encountering crawling creatures and hungry animals could have dire consequences. The stars above were my sole guide as I struggled to stay on course in the dark wilderness.

There was an abundance of knowledge to gain from the magnificently harmonious nature, which holds the highest rank in the universe-city. Amidst that awe-inspiring beauty, I had to keep my bearings precise for the journey ahead.

Somewhere along the way, a realization dawned upon me - I was no longer afraid of being alone. I was awakened with a profound sense of inner strength and contentment. Solitude was a source of growth and self-reflection that transformed into a comforting companion.

With this newfound sense of clarity and awareness, I inspected the world around me. Everything seemed more vibrant and alive, hiding its meaning within its detail and waiting to be discovered. The intricate patterns of nature, the subtle expressions of creatures, and the interconnectedness of the world are part of a perfect unity. The veil that had separated me from that unity was lifted, allowing me to see beauty in complexity.

The essence of perfection seemed to permeate

through the very atoms of every existence. I could see how the world was carefully crafted with meticulous attention to detail. From the delicate petals of a flower to the rhythmic movements of a bird in flight, the world around me showcased the exquisite beauty, purpose, and balance that existed for and within every being.

Humbled by the majesty and harmony that encapsulated everything, a restless yearning stirred within my heart. A strong desire to forge a profound connection and unlock the hidden treasures of meaning beckoned me forward. My journey was as much a self-discovery as it was an exploration before a destination. It was necessary to embrace the present moment and relish each experience as I cherished the journey in my pursuit of Truth, a path that was both challenging and rewarding.

Chapter 12 Joy of Discoveries

Exhausted and worn out, my shadow stretched out long ahead of me as I walked down the hill under the late afternoon sun.

I should have been getting close, but I had not seen a single human being for days. My water bottle was empty, and I was very thirsty. I really needed to find water soon to stay alive.

With my food and water supply long gone, I resorted to nibbling on plants to soothe my growling stomach. In front of me, there was a vast valley of wildflowers as far as my eyes could see. The fluffy clouds danced against a mastery ominous painted sky, and a shimmering silver lining added a layer of mysterious touch to the connection between the earth and the sky.

Nightfall was approaching swiftly. The melodious symphony of birds filled the air, harmonizing perfectly with the enchanting chorus of crickets. Together, their soothing music seemed to gently hush the heat vibrations of the day, creating a serene atmosphere as the day came to a close. A gentle breeze brushed against my face, carrying with it a refreshing, humid touch.

A whisper of contentment escaped my lips as I assured myself,

"Surely, there must be water nearby."

I listened carefully, drawn in by a steady, rhythmic hum that called for me to get closer.

"Is that the sound of water?" I wondered aloud.

My heart; filled with hope, anticipation, and excitement coursed through my veins. I hastened my steps; the sound of bubbling water grew ever louder. I turned sharply around a rugged hill and was greeted by a sight that exceeded all my hopes. In front of me, was a joyful scene that surpassed anything I could have imagined.

Gushing out from the rocks, the crystal-clear water flowed in a stream that quenched my thirsty throat like a dream come true. Filled with gratitude, I bent down, scooped the ice-cold water into the palm of my hand, and took a series of refreshing sips. Then I splashed the cold water over my face and neck, totally satisfied and rejuvenated.

A feeling of pure gratitude washed over me as I whispered, "Thank you, Lord, for this wonderful blessing."

With my water bottle now replenished, I continued

my journey along the stream, relishing the warm embrace of the sun. A perfect rock by the water invited me to sit down. I took off my shoes and dipped my feet into the water.

"Oh, so cold, what a magnificent therapy for my poor feet."

The gentle currents caressed my feet with a soothing sensation that felt absolutely delightful.

As my weary body sought respite, my gaze landed upon a smooth patch of ground lit by the last rays of the sun. I carefully arranged my bag into a makeshift pillow, laid down, and pulled my robe over me. Comfortably nestled in, my eyes feasted on the breathtaking scenery of that tranquil world surrounding me.

"Ah, this is perfect. All praise and gratitude be to You, the Creator of the heavens and the earth. Your creation is infinite, beautiful, and flawless. From the grandeur of the cosmos to the intricacies of the tiniest creatures. You are Worthy of all Praise."

In awe, I offered my humble praises. Thankful for the infinite marvels that surrounded me. His Divine touch permeates every essence of existence.

An enchanting display of colors painted the sky

with shades of pink and orange. Like a magical spectacle, the stars timidly emerged, gracefully joining the nighttime canvas, appearing one by one.

Dear Lord, I come before you with a humble and grateful heart, seeking Your Divine Blessings. I ask for Your Grace and Healing Power to shower upon my dear father with health and happiness. I beseech You to bless Howmi with a serene and understanding heart so that peace may prevail instead of the tensions of our siblings that should be eased now. Please lift the burdens from my mother's shoulders, calm her worries, and fill her heart with the assurance of my safety. And, Lord, above all, I implore You to envelop every one of my family in Your Divine Love that brings solace and comfort to their weary souls.

The mysterious lighting was casting a spell of ecstasy upon the world. Puffy clouds gently danced across the sky. I couldn't help but smile with each passing cloud that seemed to hold the names of my loved ones on the painted canvas: Pari, Farshawd, Farah, Howmi... Their names whispered sweet secrets from above, filling my heart with a tender, comforting warmth.

I felt a deep yearning for them, overwhelmed by waves of nostalgia that tugged at my heartstrings. Uncontrollable tears flew down my face, yet amidst it all, I found solace in the gratitude that welled up within me as I embraced the hope of a bright future ahead despite the bittersweet separation.

Oh, Lord, The Creator of the heavens and the earth, by Your Love, please heal all who suffer, bring Peace and tranquility throughout the world, and awaken the hearts of Your people to draw close to You so that they may find everlasting joy in Your Truth.

I felt a profound understanding that life itself is an eternal wellspring of love, beautifully manifested in endless and diverse forms, each serving a unique purpose, like witnessing a graceful convergence of rivers merging effortlessly as they flowed towards a magnificent and boundless ocean.

Dear Lord, I humbly ask for Your guidance to perceive the world through Your Eyes, to hear with Your Ears, and to speak with Your Words. Let me never forget that You are The One Who cradles me gently in Your loving embrace. By Your Divine Grace, I humbly request You to Honor me to serve only Your purpose.

The breathing of the life-giving flow of air nourished every cell within me. I counted the rhythmic beat of my heart that joined in a symphony of love as I drifted into a peaceful slumber and surrendered to the gentle embrace of sleep.

Chapter 13 Survival

I opened my eyes to the twinkling morning star right above me. To my right, the setting half-full moon lit the predawn sky, casting a deep blue hue that resembled a vast ocean. My empty stomach grumbled with painful hunger, but I had to wait for daylight to look for nourishment from edible plants. I stepped closer to the stream, bent over, and splashed my face and neck with its invigorating cold water. Then, put my bag around my neck and began walking downhill alongside the stream.

To my delight, I stumbled upon a fruiting prickly pear cactus grouting out of the rocks by itself, bearing ripe fruits that would placate my hunger for the next few hours. As the scorching noon sun beat down on my head, the water enticed me to take a dip. I looked around. I was certain there was no one around, but it felt strange to take off my cloth in the open. I covered my private parts with my hands before submerging into the water. It was freezing at first. Once my body adjusted, a sense of exhilaration washed over me, and I began to splash and play like a little boy.

A school of fish gracefully circled around me, seemingly intrigued by my presence. Some playfully brushed against my skin with a ticklish sensation. The mischievous side of me entertained a thought, and in an instant, I reached out and swiftly caught one of the fish in my grasp. It squirmed and wriggled before the tickling sensation let my hands open, and it slipped away and swam back into the depths.

I the playful temptation again, and this time, I caught a larger fish with both hands. With a swift motion, I emerged from the water, holding the fish tightly. It was hard to witness its struggle for life, but the thought of a warm, sustaining meal was difficult to resist. I found a sharp rock and swiftly severed its head with a single blow, aiming to minimize its pain and let the headless fish rest on a nearby rock, waiting to be prepared for a sustaining meal.

Quickly, I put on my lower body cloth. I constructed a pile of dry wood and twigs into the shape of a pyramid in a distance away from the surrounding woods. In its center, I positioned a large flat rock to serve as a heat-absorbing surface for cooking.

To ignite the fire, I picked up a large piece of stone as a handpiece and utilized a two-inch quartz I found as a striker. Soon, the flames began to dance and flicker. I reached for the wooden knife I had fashioned a few days prior, which served me well in opening and cleaning the fish's guts.

As I finished preparing the fish, the fire was ready

in a vibrant red hue. I placed the fish atop the hot, flat rock and eagerly watched it cook to perfection.

The satisfaction that enveloped me was immeasurable as I savored the hot, fresh, and unbelievably delicious meal in the midst of the untamed wilderness. The immense pleasure of tasting the flavors that danced on my taste buds nourished my being. It was a moment of pure bliss amidst the serene solitude of nature.

Thank you, Lord. I humbly ask for Your forgiveness for any unintended trespass I may have made. I am grateful for the bountiful meal You have provided and the profound experience of being in Your Magnificent Presence.

I washed the clothing I had worn under my robe since I left home and put on my only other set of clean cloth. I extinguished the remaining embers of the fire, poured water over the half-burned wood and its surroundings, and tidied the area as pristine as I had found it. Then, I filled my water bottle and hung my wet cloth on the strap of my bag to dry in the breeze. One final glance to confirm that the fire was extinguished, and its ashes were cold before embarking on the next leg of my journey with peace of mind.

Approaching nightfall, I anticipated another

breathtaking spectacle of light show to unfold before my eyes. Each sunset was a gift of a magnificent exhibition of divine verses painted in the sky with vibrant hues. Each enchantment of the mystical twilight was followed by a cast of spells of awe and wonder upon the world. An orchestrated magical testament to the majesty of creation in a perfect universe.

The radiant beacons of the stars emerged, one by one, guiding me along my path. I felt enveloped in a secure source of energy that provided me with comfort and protection. It was as though a gentle presence accompanied me with timely guidance and watchful care as I journeyed through the nights and days.

Chapter 14 A Delightful Encounter

In a state of trance, perhaps invigorated by the day's hot meal nourishment, I continued walking throughout the entire night. Venus, the morning star, radiated a heavenly glow with greeting guidance. The early birds began their slow melodies with cheerful chirping, which merged into a mesmerizing terrestrial symphony of prayers. Their joyful celebration of the sun's return marked the dawn of a fresh new day.

Surrounded by the enchanting chorus, I gazed out upon the valley that lay open before me and contemplated the distance yet to be traveled, wondering if my destination would ever come into sight.

Suddenly, I spotted something moving in the distance. Intrigued, I focused my gaze and observed people's figures traversing through the landscape. My heart fluttered with new hope as I realized that they might be able to guide me toward my destination. Excitement surged through me as I hastened my pace, eager to know what lay ahead.

Maybe I am imagining things because I'm so tired. I whispered as I ran down the hill. My vision was blurry.

I rubbed my eyes and squinted for a better focus as I curiously hurried forward to investigate.

Oh, goodness gracious! Look at all those animals - caws, sheep, and even guard dogs. So, those domestic herds most belong to someone.

I dashed with all my might, leaping over rocks, plants, and fallen trees. The idea of encountering another human filled me with excitement and anticipation. Once at the bottom of the rocky slope, I spotted someone accompanying the cattle.

That's the shepherd guiding the herd, using his staff to keep the animals together.

I shouted joyous greetings and waved my hands in the air as I ran towards him. Finally, he noticed me and waved back as he stood there looking at me, getting closer. Panting out of breath, I still couldn't contain my enthusiasm and continued to repeat joyful greetings in my overwhelming excitement.

"Hello, good morning, hello Sir, I am delightful to see you, sir! …"

To my surprise, he echoed and repeated some of the same greeting phrases I had just uttered.

"Hello, good morning, hello, Sir!"

Seeing his surprised expression, I thought he might not understand the language I was speaking. To bridge the communication gap, I began to combine gestures with my words, trying to convey my message more clearly.

Hello, Sir! My name is Behzawd, I come from Mihan, and I am on my way to Sawmawn.

His eyes widened even further, displaying a greater sense of surprise than before, as he repeated my words:

"Behzawd, Sawmawn"

He nodded his head in contemplation, placed one hand on my shoulder, and guided me with the other to walk alongside him. The warmth of his friendly touch felt comforting. Together, we made our way to a nearby tree and settled under its welcoming shade. He carefully set down his staff and untied a bundle that was hanging at its end. He unwrapped it and laid out pieces of bread, cheese, and a few dates. With a cheerful smile, he invited me to partake in the delightful feast.

"Breakfast, you, hungry, tired, eat, please," he kindly offered.

Overwhelmed with gratitude, I felt like jumping up

and kissing him to express my appreciation.

"We speak almost the same language," I exclaimed with heartfelt joy.

Although his words resembled a strong dialect of my language, we were able to communicate with each other. The homemade bread was the most delicious meal on its own. He talked as we ate while his flocks grazed nearby.

"I am familiar with Sawmawn but not Mihan," he remarked.

I let out a joyous scream out of excitement.

"That is all I need!"

With his index finger, he pointed in a specific direction.

"See those mountains?"

I nodded.

"Yes, yes."

"Sawmawn is over there, behind those mountains, a long journey ahead," he explained.

His friendly companionship filled my heart with warmth and comfort.

"You must rest. Difficult mountains to pass through; stay here tonight," he kindly advised.

"Thank you, but I don't want to impose on you," I responded with gratitude.

"No bother at all. You can leave early in the morning," he assured me.

His kind offer was genuine as if it emanated from his sincere goodwill.

"You are my God sent angel. Thank you. Perhaps resting here will give me a better chance of reaching my destination with renewed energy," I gratefully expressed.

For the remainder of the day, we herded the flocks, talked, and enjoyed the remaining food for lunch. His beautiful, young, and playful German Shepherd was his expert assistant in keeping the herds under control. As the afternoon sun began to cast longer shadows, we guided the animals back towards their home.

Once the animals were herded into the barn, he closed the gates and placed his hand on my shoulder as we walked towards his farmhouse. In the front yard, a young woman was gathering laundry from clotheslines. As we approached, two children, about 5 and 8 years old, ran towards us to greet the shepherd with excitement.

"Baba, baba, Hello, baba!"

With a voice filled with love and affection, he greeted them, lifted the younger one into his arms, and knelt to embrace the other. "Hello, my darling little ones," as he caressed them and gazed into their eyes one at a time.

After a few moments, he let lose his embrace on the children, who turned their curious gazes towards me, the stranger standing next to their father. Their inquisitive expressions seemed to seek an explanation for my presence.

The lady picked up the last piece of clothing from the line and joined everyone walking into the building.

"Peace and Blessings, dear," he kindly tried to take a load of cloth from her while turning towards me. "My wife, Nadima."

"Hello, Lady Nadima! I am honored to meet you."

"Hello, Sir! Welcome!"

"Thank you, dear lady, my name is Behzawd, I apologize for imposing,"

I felt like I was intruding on their family's private time.

The children's excitement grew as they repeated to perfect their pronunciation of my name.

"Behzawd, Behzawd, welcome, Sir Behzawd!" they exclaimed in unison with warm, enthusiastic voices.

The young girl couldn't contain her joy any longer and had to talk to share her happiness with everyone.

"My name is Nina, Sir Behzawd, and my brother's is Simeon."

I extended my hand towards her for a handshake.

"I am honored to meet you, Ms. Nina."

Then, I turned to her brother.

"It is truly a pleasure to meet you, Master Simeon."

The children found a sheer delight in our exchanged dialogue and energetically bound up the stairs, their peals of conversation interwoven with laughter echoed through the air.

I felt a sense of comfort and belonging in their presence. His gentle demeanor, akin to that of an older brother, enveloped me in a warm embrace. The joyful smiles on their faces mirrored the warmth and hospitality that radiated from their hearts. They were genuinely happy to have a visitor, and I was ecstatic to find myself in their welcoming home. A warm, friendly connection had blossomed between us only in a matter of few moments.

Lady Nadima excused herself and ascended the stairs to join her children inside. The shepherd kindly gestured for me to go first. I declined, and he took my hand and led us up together. We passed the veranda and entered a small room that emanated a simple and peaceful family life. Love radiated from every object that was meticulously placed by dedicated, caring hands. The children's eyes sparkled with curiosity in their youthful wonder.

"Common, Sir Behzawd, come and sit here."

His wife blushed as she watched their joyful enthusiasm.

"They mean our home is yours, Sir Behzawd. New faces are a rare sight for us, and please make yourself comfortable."

She gestured with her hand, inviting me to take a seat on any of the benches surrounding the table in the center of the room. I settled onto the nearest bench, and the children were quick to sit by my sides, looking at me with curiosity.

"Where did you come from, Sir Beh... umm?" the

boy struggled.

"Behzawd," Nina helped.

"Thank you, dear ones, I came from Mihan,"

"Where is Mihan? Is it far?"

Their father chuckled with affection.

"Mihan must be far away, my children. Even I am not familiar with it! Plus, Sir Behzawd has been traveling for quite some time. I can imagine he must be very tired."

His wife set the table and served the dinner as we talked.

"You must be hungry, Sir!"

"Oh, no, dear lady," I replied gratefully, "your generous husband shared his breakfast and lunch with me. It was absolutely delicious and more than enough to keep me satisfied throughout the day."

The family made me feel right at home.

"That was breakfast, Behzawd, many hours ago." he clarified with a warm smile.

Laughter filled the room as the shepherd broke the bread. He graciously began serving the meal, starting with me. He placed a generous portion of roasted lamb and creamy mashed potatoes on a beautiful clay plate before me. Then, he served the children, his wife, and himself. We all bowed our heads in reverence as the young Nina took the lead in saying a prayer of gratitude.

"Thank You, Lord, for Your abundant blessings, for our loving family, for Sir Behzawd, and for Your infinite love that surrounds us. We are grateful for the food before us. We humbly pray that You provide nourishment for all those who are hungry. All praises belong to You, our Lord. Amin."

"Amin," everyone repeated.

The food was absolutely delicious. Everyone enjoyed the meal in a peaceful silence interrupted only by the delightful sounds of utensils against clay plates. The children finished their food first, anxious to engage in conversation.

"Sir Behzawd, would you stay with us for a while?" Nina asked with hopeful anticipation.

"I'm sorry, dear," I replied gently, "I have to go to Sawmawn."

"Will you come back?" with a touch of longing in her voice.

"Perhaps,"

I nodded with a smile, not wanting to disappoint her.

"One day, it might just be possible."

After everyone finished eating, the lady graciously cleared the table while the husband excused himself and stepped out of the room. Meanwhile, the children took turns keeping me engaged with their curious questions.

Soon, the shepherd returned, carrying blankets and bedding supplies. He skillfully arranged a cozy bed near the window at the other end of the room. Once finished, he rejoined us at the table, taking a seat with a warm smile.

"That bed is for you," the shepherd said with a warm smile. "I hope it is comfortable."

"Thank you, Sir," I replied gratefully. "I am sure it will be heavenly and far more comfortable than the makeshift beds I have been using in the wild."

We laughed. The children joined in with their innocent giggles, but they didn't quite understand what was so funny.

"Now, children, it's getting late," their mother

reminded them. "Let's go to bed so that Sir Behzawd can get a good night's rest."

"Will you still be here in the morning, Sir Behzawd?" asked Nina.

"Not when you wake up," I replied with a warm smile.

"Oh, why not? Please stay."

"I must go to find my uncle. But we will meet again if God Pleases. I really enjoyed meeting you guys."

"Me too," Nina said sincerely.

"Me too," her brother followed.

"We will miss you. Good night, Sir Behzawd."

"I will miss you too. I hope you have sweet dreams tonight, will you?"

"Okay, thank you," said Nina.

"Okay, thank you," mimicked her brother.

"Good night, Sir."

"Good night."

"Thank you for your hospitality. May God Bless your home with everlasting love and happiness."

"Thank you, Sir. Good night, and safe journey," said Lady Nadima as she guided the kids out the door to the adjacent room.

"Rest well, Behzawd. Good night." said the shepherd and followed them.

They left the room. It had been ages since I rested on a cozy, comfortable, and plush bed. I drifted off into a serene slumber within moments and slept deep through the night.

Chapter 15 Goodbye

As the rooster's call pierced through the air, I sprang out of bed with a jolt. Momentarily disoriented. It took a few seconds to familiarize myself with my surroundings. Memories of the previous day and the companionship of my newfound friend eased my mind. Swiftly, I gathered and folded the bedding sheets and stacked them neatly against the wall. Grabbing my bag with utmost caution so as not to disturb the peaceful morning, I quietly stepped onto the veranda, ready to embrace the day.

The shepherd and his family had been incredibly warm and generous hosts. With gratitude in my heart, I decided to wait a little while longer to bid them farewell.

Standing there on the veranda, lost in the majestic beauty of the mountains that resembled sculpted figures, I felt the eager anticipation of once again venturing into their embrace in pursuit of my intended destination. A soft murmuring of a distant stream faintly reached my ears, adding to the harmonious symphony of nature in that enchanting scenery.

I wondered how much longer it would be until the shepherd awoke to start his day.

Up above, Venus shone radiant while Mars gracefully nestled beneath it. A humble little star, Jupiter, graced above Venus. Sporadic calls from awakening birds and other creatures reverberated off the lofty mountains. A symphony of nature was awakening. The north direction that the shepherd had pointed to for my destination lay to my left, beckoning me toward new adventures.

"Peace and Blessings"

my host had just stepped out.

"Good morning, Sir! Peace and Blessings to you as well!"

"Did you sleep well?"

"Oh, yes, Sir, I rested very well, thank you. I am ready to run through those mountains."

He smiled and gently put his hand on my shoulder.

"I am glad to hear that. You are young and full of energy. Surely, you can run through those mountains."

We both smiled. His words were heartwarming.

My thoughts were consumed with finding a way to show my gratitude since I woke up. Hesitant for fear of offending him, I pulled a valuable coin from my robe's pocket and discreetly nestled it into his palm.

"This is not worth much; please accept this little as a token of my gratitude, please!"

Gracefully, he guided my fingers to close my fist and respectfully moved my hand aside.

"Oh, Behzawd, it has been an incredible honor to have you grace us with your presence! God has been Most Gracious to send you to visit us! Not many people venture this way. I hope we meet again, my dear friend."

I was lost for words.

"Meeting you and your beautiful family has been an absolute pleasure, Sir. Your gracious hospitality has filled my heart with warmth and strength. It saddens me to have to bid farewell."

He raised his hand gently, signaling for a brief pause

"Please wait a moment," he kindly requested and hurried inside.

After a few minutes, he came back with a bundle.

"You have a long journey ahead of you. This should help a little," he said with a warm smile as he handed it to me.

"Thank you so much. How can I ever repay you?"

I asked with heartfelt gratitude.

Observing my speechless embarrassment, "There's no need to repay me. Just pay it forward, my friend."

Then, he put his hand on my shoulder and pointed to the left across the valley.

"Sawmawn is right over there, just beyond those mountains. You'll need to cross three ranges to reach it. You see, it's right over there,"

His words filled me with renewed energy and determination as "Right over there" echoed in my mind, instilling a resounding belief that my destination was well within reach.

"I won't miss it, thank you, Sir. I would have loved to stay until everyone wakes up to say farewell, but I must get on the way. God Willing, perhaps our paths will cross again in the future,"

"Yes, God Willing, we may indeed, you have a safe journey, my friend."

Our embrace felt like saying goodbye to a dear old friend.

"Please convey my gratitude to your kind family."

"I shall," he assured me with a nod.

My heart was filled to the brim with gratitude.

"May God Bliss all of you,"

"May God be with you,"

I made my way down the stairs as I reciprocated well wishes,

"Peace and Blessings".

Chapter 16 The Awakened Soul

I felt the warmth of the shepherd's hand on my shoulder throughout the remainder of my journey when I thought about it. His humble hospitality had uplifted my spirit and rejuvenated my energy.

As the sun reached its highest point in the sky, I remained undeterred by its relentless heat. Instead, I sang praises and joined the singing birds that echoed through the air. I sang praises along with the birds and paused from time to time to listen to the echoes bouncing off the surrounding mountains. Then, I let my voice soar again with the birds in a symphony of joyful praises.

"Perhaps the birds do the same when they pause for a moment of respite," I mused, imagining the feathered creatures conducting their own symphony in that grand amphitheater.

Being indulged in the experience of the moments was free from worries. What was otherwise ordinary sounds of nature took on a surreal and magical quality. The chirping of birds became a symphony of enchanting melodies, the rustling of leaves transformed into whispers of ancient secrets, and the gentle breeze carried whispers of ethereal whispers.

The world around me had transformed into a realm of wonder and beauty, filled with extraordinary creatures and unseen wonders, all waiting to be discovered in the magic of the present moment.

Despite moments of fear and uncertainty, the unknown path ahead filled me with a thrilling sense of excitement. The element of surprise and the anticipation of what awaited me around each corner kept me fully aware and engaged with my surroundings. Each thrilling adventure became an opportunity for discovery and personal growth that surpassed my wildest dreams.

Navigating through challenges and surviving each obstacle not only left me with a profound sense of fulfillment, but also opened my eyes to a better understanding of the vast and intricate realms of spirituality beyond the mundane. Like an awakening, it deepened my inner connection with the unseen. I realized how necessary my journey was for my discovery of the intertwined physical and spiritual possibilities.

I had walked non-stop since dawn. Now, engulfed by a breathtaking panoramic, I found myself in a peaceful world bathed in the warm, gentle glow of the setting sun. It was a scene that compelled me to sit in awe and observe its serene beauty. Vibrant hues of orange and red painted the sky, each brushstroke imbued with the whispers of stories woven through the passage of time.

"Ah, this is perfect; I need to refurbish my energy!" I exclaimed joyfully as I gently untied the corners of the bundle that the kind shepherd had handed me. The content was adorned with delightful portions of the delicious food he had shared with me the day before - homemade bread, cheese, and an abundance of sweet dates that would last me for days. I happily indulged in enough to satisfy my hunger.

"Thank you, dear Lord. May your blessings overflow for the Shepherd and his family."

With a grateful heart, I wrapped up the bundle and laid down on my back.

I marveled at the puffy silver lined clouds dancing swiftly with the last traces of orange and red hues. My breath was a gentle whisper of love, prayer, and gratitude. A soft breeze caressed my nostrils, carrying with it a delicate, sweet fragrance of wildflowers.

"Oh, dear Lord, is this all a dream? Was I lost in slumber before this moment? Your wonders are truly endless. Everything bears witness to Your magnificent creation. Even this seemingly lifeless stone upon which I lie serves a grand purpose. The molecules of air suspended around me shimmer with unseen beauty... Oh, Lord, I offer my sincere praise to You, and You only. How can one ever begin to count the obvious blessings You have bestowed upon each one of Your creations freely? Your hidden blessings are even more vast and profound than what eyes can perceive.

I am grateful to You for guiding me to the kind shepherd, Your devoted servant. Only through Your divine teachings have I witnessed unique and indescribable signs. I humbly ask that You shower him and his family with Your abundant bounties. Thank You, Lord, for my own family. Thank You for my dear father, for my ever-loving mother. Please grant my father complete health and well-being, and, please, bring healing and peace to my entire family.

I seek Your forgiveness for my shortcomings. I have been ensnared by the trivial disputes and worries of this world like a foolish soul. Please heal my dear brother, Howmi, and fill his heart with Your boundless love. Keep my beloved Farah close to Your presence. Grant her patience and wisdom. Only You Know the souls who have played a part in guiding me to submit to Your Will. Please Bless them with Your eternal Love..."

A profound longing to surrender to God's Will

consumed my entire being with a sense of purpose and peace. Though my lips became weary and unable to utter a sound, my heart, pulsing veins, every breath, and even my very bones were crying out in praise. The entire universe joined in to unite me with the graceful current of blessings that carried me away in a joyous river of adoration.

"Oh, You, The Creator of the heavens and the earth, Your beauty knows no bounds, love emanates from Your essence, You are Adorned with the most beautiful Names, I humbly seek Your forgiveness for my lack of understanding, please keep me close to You, enveloped in Your Merciful Presence, guide me to remain steadfast on the path of Truth and righteousness, shelter me within Your boundless grace..."

I drifted off into a peaceful slumber while my words remained unfinished.

Chapter 17 Heaven on Earth

Opening my eyes, I felt light and weightless, almost like floating in a vast expanse of space. Something greater than life embraced me with infinite possibilities that united me with the whole universe.

In front of me were twinkling stars surrounding the glowing full moon. The summer creatures played their surreal symphony. I remembered the wonderful feelings of happiness and bliss before I had fallen asleep.

Suddenly, I was struck by a realization - the moon had been full on that night when I left home and embarked on this journey of solitude.

"Wow! I have been traveling for a whole month," I whispered, amazed by the passage of time.

As I sat up straight bathed in the moonlight, I saw a deep mysterious world unfold before me. The earth and sky were intertwined in awe-inspiring beauty. I could not help but bow down in humble reverence and prostration.

For a whole month, I encountered so many incredible moments that I couldn't have experienced in a lifetime. I had walked under the ethereal lighting of the moon that guided me on my earthly path while filling my soul with the joy of becoming. The universe seemed to be cheering me on and aligned its forces to give me everything I needed to forge forward despite all the uncertainties.

"Dear God, Glory be Unto You. Truly, You have created all this for a purpose; I kindly ask for Your forgiveness for my ignorance in leaving my family, for not realizing the value of my loved ones, for taking their presence for granted ... but I realize now that I would have remained ignorant of all this had I not left home. Thank You for every breath You Grant me, as long as it serves Your purpose. Please guide me to make the most of each breath and not waste this precious gift."

My heart was singing praises like dancing with the universe.

"Oh, my dear Lord, Praise belongs to You, Oly You, The Creator of majesty and beauty in heavens, the earth, and all in between, The Most Gracious One, The Most Merciful One, I surrender myself to You, you are my Master, to You I turn, in You, I seek refuge …"

I stood up and gathered my little belongings, "Oh Lord, I trust in You; there is no might and no power but in You," I whispered as I ventured forward beneath the enchanting moonlight. It was as bright as daylight. From that night onward, I collected a precious pebble every day to help me keep track of the days of my journey onward.

In the days and nights that followed, I walked with renewed energy, never ceasing my steps except for brief pauses to catch my breath. I traversed through the next two mountain ranges, defying the scorching heat of the sun and the playful hide-and-seek games of the moon behind passing clouds. Nothing could deter me from marching onwards.

In the soft, mystical light of dawn, the shimmering morning stars bid farewell to the fading crescent moon. Weary from days of walking with little rest, I rounded a bend. Suddenly, a breathtaking panorama view unfolded right before my eyes. The beauty was so serene, so ethereal, that it felt more like a realm of fairies and enchantment than a place on earth. I couldn't help but be captivated, in awe of the magical world that presented itself before my tired eyes.

"What an incredible place to find on earth! Could this be an enchanted fairyland? Have I transcended to another realm of existence? Or was this the gateway to my long-awaited destination?" I whispered in sheer amazement, "Perhaps I have entered the realm of earthly mystics or even life after death."

Spellbound by the sight, I pinched myself to confirm it was all real. The words of the shepherd echoed in my ears: "you cannot miss it!". He mentioned that he knew about Sawmawn. So, he might have been here himself! This extraordinary sanctuary may have been what he was referring to as such. My destination may be within my reach now.

I counted the pebbles in my pocket.

"… eight, nine, ten." Altogether, I figured I had traveled for forty days.

A sweet air brushed against my face like a breeze of glad tidings. Fueled by joy, gratitude, and a sense of wonder, I forged ahead with renewed excitement. Skipping down the rocky path, my eyes were drawn to a flickering light in the distance. Its glow urged me to quicken my pace.

People live there. This could very well be the land where Uncle Kia resides.

The thought energized me even more in my spirited run down the final stretch of rocky terrain. The distant shimmering light disappeared as the sunlight intensified. In the embrace of the orange-red sky, the valley's scenery was adorned with a captivating array of colors. The birds chirped their delightful songs like the finishing touches to their morning symphony.

The valley was surrounded by mountains on three sides. Many waterfalls cascaded down like narrow white drapes. The tranquil sounds fille the air with an ethereal melody. The highest peak glistened with a pristine coat of snow. A mysterious pull beckoned me forward, inviting me to partake in the celebration of a new chapter of my journey.

"This must be reminiscent of, if not akin to heaven itself, so magnificent, Oh Lord ..."

At the skirts of the mountains, graceful rivers meandered and divided the lush green land into distinct sections.

"Those must be orchards of a variety of fruits." I talked to myself in awe as my eyes feasted upon the beautiful scenery.

In search of refreshment to satisfy my thirst, I approached the nearby stream. Crystal-clear water flowed swiftly over its smooth and glossy stone bed. I leaned over and extended my arm to scoop some water to drink. Short of reaching the water, I took another step.

Suddenly, I was startled by a creature lurking

below. I swiftly retreated and scanned my surroundings for any changes. Nothing unusual. With cautious curiosity, I approached the edge again, peering down to get a closer look at the mysterious thing. I met with the gaze of a face adorned with wide, scary eyes, long hair, and tattered clothing. It took a few seconds before I burst into laughter.

"What a terrifying appearance!" I looked utterly more dreadful than some of the wild creatures I had encountered in the wild. "People would surely flee in terror if they were to lay eyes on me."

Feeling weary and disheartened, I sat down to find a solution to my current predicament. In the distance, a lively scene of people and animals bustling about in their various activities was unfolding.

"Could anyone out there possibly know my uncle's whereabouts?" I wondered.

Determined to find out, I returned to the stream to freshen up and improve my unkempt appearance. I washed my face and head. The cool water rejuvenated my skin as I used my fingers as a makeshift comb and carefully arranged and braided my hair, pulling it back neatly. Then, I gazed into the water and found a reflection that was less intimidating than before.

I should be careful not to startle people, a stranger

in tattered clothes with this jarring look … I whispered, "Oh dear Lord, please Guide our encounter and bless us with friendship and understanding."

Motivated by a strong sense of determination, I began to walk briskly, almost running, towards the active figures in the distance.

Chapter 18 Holy Grounds

Animals grazed in the pasture fields across the orchards with busy fruit pickers. I raised my hands in the air to attract someone's attention. With a joyful voice, I greeted them, but to my dismay, they remained unaware of my presence. Determined not to startle or worry them, I kept my hand waving up in the air to express my peaceful intentions.

"Hello … Peace … Blessings … Hi"

At last, someone took notice of me and paused his work. With a friendly wave of his hand, he acknowledged my presence before going back to his business. I continued my greetings. He paused again, perplexed, perhaps pondering upon my presence since I was not one of them. I contained my excitement and kept one hand waving in the air to show that I meant no harm.

"Hello there! I come in peace," I reassured with a warm, genuine voice. It was important to alleviate any concerns or fears that may have arisen with my presence.

Getting closer, I remained calm with one hand resting on my heart as a sign of respect and honor and the other raised in the air. It was essential to establish a connection that would foster trust and understanding.

"Hello, greetings, Peace"

The man repeated my greeting words.

"Hello. Greetings, Peace"

Happy to see other humans but doubtful if they could understand my language, I repeated the same greeting words, hoping to convey my genuine sincerity without causing any alarm.

"Hello, Peace"

As I approached, a few other farmers gathered around the first man and stood together, observing me with curious eyes. I was determined to make a friendly connection. With a warm smile, I continued my calm approach to show my goodwill, still repeating my greetings.

"Hello… Peace… Blessing to you"

beaming with happiness, I eagerly shook their hands. Their friendly reception was overwhelming. The way they repeated my greetings with such precision made me wonder if they truly grasped the meaning behind the words. Nevertheless, I focused my attention on understanding their words. To bridge any communication gaps, I combined expressed my words with hand gestures and body language to establish a connection as I articulated the words slowly.

"I … want … to … go … to … Sawmawn. I … am … looking … for … Sir Kia ... Do … you … know … Sir Kia?"

"Yes, yes."

Seeing their collective nodding, I couldn't help but feel a slight sense of doubt. It seemed that my question may not have been fully understood. With patience, I had to come up with an alternative to overcome our language barrier with visual cues or simpler phrases.

"Sawmawn?"

"Yes"

"Sir Kia?"

"Yes, Sir Kia, yes,"

They nodded yes, again and again.

But it seemed too good to be true. I was confused when they all talked at the same time, mixed with simultaneous chatter.

I raised my hand gently to signal for a moment of pause. Turning towards the man who had initially noticed me and was standing by my side, I addressed him directly.

"Please… say… it… slow... Do… you… know… Sir Kia?"

He began to speak slowly, too, one word at a time.

"Yes … Here … Sawmawn ... Sir Kia … is our … great … protecting … father ... He … owns … this … land … everything … here ... His … father … Sir Zia … His … brother in-law … Farshawd … son of … Farsaw"

He left no room for doubt in my mind with his detailed and accurate summary of Uncle Kia's ancestry. Referring to him as father revealed a deep and sincere respect for him. Although this brought a sense of relief, my heart yearned for more reassurance. To fulfill this longing within me, I posed more questions to confirm my understanding.

"Sir Kia, is your father?"

Everybody volunteered excited opinions.

"Ya! Ya! Good father"

"He owns this land?"

"Ya! Ya! Everything"

Their collective agreement, sincerity, respect, and

trust for Uncle as their father was heartwarming. The same farmer placed his hand on my shoulder and spoke in deliberate, slow words.

"Listen brother, Prophet Farsaw was… grandfather of Sir Kia's wife, peace be upon them. He was… born… and chosen… to prophecy… right here, on this land. His fathers lived here before him. He was raised high above all mankind. He brought… blessings… to this land."

I noticed his facial features were lined with the graceful passage of time yet radiating a sun-kissed glow. Plus, the touch of his hand on my shoulder conveyed a sense of security that enhanced our communication.

"Thank you, brother. I am so very happy to be here," he said, looking him in the eyes when he stopped talking.

"I was filled with eager anticipation as I set out to locate my dear uncle. Gratitude and admiration swirled in my mind for The One who guided me on this quest to find one of His devoted servants."

With a heart filled gratitude, I gazed at everyone and spoke, "May God's blessings and abundant prosperity be upon you all. Peace and blessings to the messengers of God, who have graced you, their followers, with faith and unwavering dedication."

"Amin. God bless you. You are a blessing from God to come here to visit our land."

We conversed with deliberate, slow pronunciation, accompanied by body language that appeared to be effective.

Then, as if extending an invitation, they gestured towards the farmhouses in the distant land.

"Please, let's head there; you are most welcome to our homes."

"Thank you, brothers. I am honored to be in your midst."

humbled by their uplifting offer, yet anxious to learn more about Uncle's whereabouts:

"You are incredibly hospitable to a stranger like me. God bless you all. Could you please tell me where Sir Kia lives?"

They responded together, "We will take you there."

then, a group of seven began to move. The first farmer placed his hand on my back, guiding me to walk alongside him. After a few steps, I turned and halted, facing them,

"Gentlemen, my brothers in faith, I am grateful for your hospitality. I do not wish to disrupt your important work any further. These farms and herds rely on your care. I would appreciate it if you could only guide me on how to get there."

Disappointed, they exclaimed in unison, "It's not far. We'll escort you there.'

"I am truly honored. Thank you, brothers. Please, just provide me with directions."

Responding to my request, the first farmer at my side placed his hand on my back and gestured across the fields with his other hand, saying, "Do you see that large white building over there?"

"Yes"

"Sir Kia lives there. You can't miss it. I can go with you."

It was hard to believe that Uncle Kia was so close. "Oh, no. I will go myself. Please go back to your work."

I hastily shook his hand, then bowed to the group with one hand placed on my chest to express my gratitude. As I began to walk away, I waved goodbye to them.

Energized with excitement, I broke into a run, feeling my heart pounding loudly in my chest. The thought that my uncle lived there and that I was so close to seeing him and his family was almost unbelievable. The anticipation of the reunion filled me with joy.

As I neared the white building, three dogs suddenly burst into barking in unison from inside behind a grand wooden gateway.

"Hello, fellows!" I called out in a surprised yet amused voice, which seemed to add to their excitement.

They stared at me like vigilant guards at their posts, their barking persisting as I advanced closer.

"Hello, beautiful. Could you kindly inform your master that you have a visitor?"

They began to calm down, the barking subsiding as if they were negotiating something. Suddenly, one of the dogs made a noise that seemed like it was announcing a decision to the others. It swiftly darted back through the orchard-lined yard and vanished from my sight, leaving the remaining two to stand guard in silence.

"You are doing a great job, beautiful. I hope I'm

not causing any disturbance for your master..."

Chapter 19 New Home

A s I stood at the gate, my heart filled with anticipation, imagining the moment when I would finally jump into my uncle's arms.

Questions lingered in my mind: "could anyone notice my presence here? Who would come to receive me? Would it be Uncle?"

How I long to embrace him in my arms. Oh, Lord, grant me the strength to bring joy and happiness to his household.

As the missing dog came bounding from the far corner of the yard, barking with excitement, my attention was drawn to the figure of a person emerging from the same spot. A sense of constriction gripped me as if my very skin was pulling me apart. I observed the tall figure, a young girl, moving with elegance. Overwhelmed by self-consciousness and embarrassment, I stood tensely, averting my gaze to the ground so as not to intrude upon her presence. At that moment, all the words I possessed seemed to escape me.

"Oh, Lord, guide me to not disturb the peace of this household. Perhaps this is not Uncle Kia's home after all."

Dressed in a light-colored overall, she was accompanied by the dogs as they ran and walked beside her until they reached the gate. Standing at roughly my height, I felt a wave of apology wash over me, my words tumbling out in a jumbled mumble.

"Peace and blessings, ma'am. Please forgive my intrusion. My name is Behzawd, and I have traveled from Mihan in search of my uncle, Sir Kia."

I felt foolish. Why would she care about any of that?

When she heard my name, she smiled and swung the gates open wide.

"And to you, Peace and Blessings as well, Sir. Behzawd. Please, come in."

With a swift, thankful glance in her direction, I entered.

"Thank you, ma'am."

Before proceeding inside, I needed to confirm if this was indeed the right place.

"Do you know Sir Kia, ma'am?"

She smiled.

"My father is inside. Please, come in."

I entered as she closed the gates behind me and began to walk away.

"Please, come."

I followed behind, my mind struggling to process a jumble of confusing thoughts. "Could it be that Uncle Kia is her father?"

As we strolled through the orchard-lined yard, we made our way to a stunning garden. From where she had emerged, we entered the picturesque courtyard. In the center, a pool mirrored the white stucco columns of the building's open veranda. The air was filled with the familiar scents of flowers and fruits, evoking memories of home.

Her graceful stride brought to mind the elegance of my mother's walk. "Oh, mother."

Suddenly, a wave of emotions overwhelmed me. Panicked by my thoughts, I swiftly wiped my eyes.

"Lord, I seek refuge in You from my weaknesses. Please forgive my trespasses. Grant me the strength to conceal my pain and bring happiness to this household, not sorrow."

As I observed the masterful arrangement of flowers and the serene setting in the garden, my focus shifted to the present moment. The joyful melodies of the singing birds further emphasized the divine presence that surrounded us.

"Oh, my Lord, thank You! With You, I lack nothing; without You, I have nothing. I could not have envisioned this beautiful destination in my long and lonely journey. By Your grace, all things are possible. You are the One Who is all Knowing all Powerful."

Her excited call of 'Bawbaw, Bawbaw' startled me out of my thoughts.

Once we reached the front of the building, she ascended the stairs. "Bawbaw"

she stepped inside. I slowly climbed up the stairs to give her space, waiting on the veranda. Within moments, a tall, white-haired, jolly man rushed out and enveloped me in a warm embrace.

"Peace and Blessings, Behzawd, welcome son, welcome."

His facial features bore a striking resemblance to those of my mother's.

"Peace… Uncle… Uncle Kia… My Uncle…"

Speechless, I held onto him.

"My Uncle… My dear Uncle…"

It was difficult to believe I was actually there. I felt the urge to cry. It had been a while since I had experienced such emotions.

He wrapped my shoulders with one of his mighty arms and led us inside. I held onto him like a child, wrapping my arm around his waist. As we walked through various rooms, engaging in conversation, we occasionally glanced at each other in astonishment, laughing heartily as we entered a room where the ladies warmly greeted me. Joyful Uncle rested his free hand on my chest:

"Here is Behzawd, my beloved nephew."

"Welcome… Welcome…"

the ladies repeated warmly as he introduced them:

"Do you remember lady Banoo, my wife?"

"Yes, Peace and Blessings, ma'am."

"Zivar, my daughter"

"Peace and Blessings, miss."

"You have already met my Negawr."

"Peace and Blessings, miss."

"And, here is Lady Nadim."

"Peace and Blessings, ma'am"

I bowed to each lady with my hand on my chest. I later learned that Nadim was the family's trusted maid. With a warm welcome and genuine happiness, they accepted me as one of their own. Banoo broke the cycle of repeated greetings.

"Dearest Behzawd, what an honor to have you with us! What a pleasant surprise. You must be tired and thirsty! Would you care for some milk?

Her smile lifted the lines of her cheeks, and her rounded brows accentuated her kind, happy eyes.

"Thank you, Ma'am. It's wonderful to be here with you. Yes, please, milk sounds great. Thank you."

Accepting her offer was the least I could do to show my gratitude for their warm reception. With a quick glance at Nadim, she continued,

"How was your trip? Did you travel with a caravan? How long have you been travelling?"

Before she finished her questions, Nadim came back and placed a cup of milk on a plate in front of me.

A table was set for breakfast by the windows. Uncle sat at the head of the table across from Banoo. He invited me with the gesture of his hand to take the seat to his right, across from Negawr, with Zivar by her side. He laughed with joy, frequently glancing at me in disbelief.

"You are just in time for breakfast, my son. Let us begin… in the Name of God, The Most Beneficent, The Most Merciful."

Everyone repeated.

"In the Name of God, The Most Beneficent, The Most Merciful." after the first few moments of quiet, conversations began with questions that were difficult to hold back, and they continued until everyone had finished breakfast.

Uncle's pressing questions were about his sister and everyone else.

"How was Pari… Farshawd… Farah… Howmi…"

The colorful light rays that filtered through the stained-glass windowpanes amplified the radiant glow of happiness on their faces.

I felt lightheaded and dizzy despite the joy, struggling to keep my eyelids open after eating. I made an effort to stay alert out of courtesy, but my body was not cooperating. My struggle was probably more apparent than I realized, as Uncle Kia showed sympathy when I stopped eating:

"You must be very tired, my son."

Nadim was sitting next to me on my right, between me and Banoo. She left the room after Banoo whispered something to her, then turned to look at me.

"I hope you will be comfortable here, Behzawd. Please make it your home. Ask for anything you need."

Nadim had returned and was standing at the doorway.

"Nadim will show you to your room. You need to rest. We'll catch up when you're feeling more rested."

Immensely grateful for her understanding, I managed to pull myself up to stand on my tired feet.

"Thank you, Ma'am. Please excuse my fatigue. It is an honor to be with you all."

Not wanting to keep Nadim waiting, I tried to hide my limping, sore legs. I hugged Uncle Kia, bowed to the ladies, and followed her.

She walked sideways in front of me to avoid turning her back to me. When we reached an opening with steps leading down to the courtyard, she pointed to another opening across the yard.

"The restroom is right there."

"Oh, okay, thank you."

We continued down the hallway past the steps. She stopped to open a door and stepped to the side to let me enter first.

The room was spacious. Walls and niches were carefully decorated with beautiful, delicate objects. I later learned that they were all handcrafted by Zivar and Negawr.

"You can ring the bell for me by pulling on this."

She showed me the wooden handle connected to a rope hanging from the ceiling.

"I am always nearby; it takes a couple of minutes for me to get here."

"Thank you, lady Nadim."

"You are most welcome, Sir. Do you need anything?"

"No, thank you. This is perfect."

"I hope you rest well, Sir. Peace and Blessings."

She stepped out and closed the door behind her.

The bed near the window was impossible to resist. I walked up to the bed, where a fabulous view of the garden was inviting, but my brain was too tired to give it much thought.

Beyond the apparent reasons, a profound sense of happiness enveloped me despite my being tired. Every ounce of energy had deserted me; even shedding my robe seemed an insurmountable task. I collapsed on the bed and drifted unconscious before I could gather my thoughts.

Chapter 20 A Sense of Purpose

Roused by the rooster's clarion call, I awoke to find the room's dim twilight a stark departure from the untamed vastness of the open wild.

What a dream that was... arriving at Uncle Kia's homestead, embraced by the warmth of his family's presence, a tapestry of kinship woven with threads of nostalgia."

The soft serenade of dawn's early birds beckoned, drawing my gaze toward the window where the first hints of daylight whispered through.

"Oh, this is no dream. I am truly at Uncle Kia's abode, the rooster's call heralding the dawn. How long have I slept? A full cycle of day and night! What a lapse in decorum, especially on my first day.

Swiftly, I slipped into the fresh clothes I had laundered a few days prior, tidied my bed with haste, and stole out of the room in silence. The house was still. Not a soul in sight. I made my way down into the courtyard with the location of the restroom etched in my memory.

Amidst the garden's tranquil lighting at dawn, I approached the central pool, where I cleansed my hands and face, readying myself for prayer. The twinkling morning star reflected like a celestial jewel that was brought within my reach. My whispered praises echoed through the quiet splendor as I retraced back into the building with gentle steps.

"Oh, Lord. You are Great. Greater than can be explained or imagined, You are pure, You are The One, Worthy of all Praise... Praise unto You."

Walking in the hallway towards the breakfast room. I noticed an open door and listened. I heard Uncle Kia praying. I saluted quietly before entering to let my presence be known.

"Peace... Blessings..."

Waited for a few seconds. I knew when Uncle was praying, he wouldn't answer and probably wouldn't mind if I joined him. With a little louder salutation, I entered.

"Peace and Blessing to you."

Uncle's silhouette framed against the window drew me closer. I walked over, stood behind him and prayed quietly. In a state of total ecstasy, we were lost in our own worlds, standing, bowing, and prostrating, until the room was bathed in the brilliance of full daylight.

We had been immersed in meditation for some

time when he turned to acknowledge my presence.

"Peace and blessings, my son. May your prayers be accepted."

"Peace and blessing to you, Uncle. May God accept yours as well."

"How are you, my son? Did you sleep well?"

"I am very well, Uncle. Praise God, I slept too well through a whole day and night."

"You needed the rest, my son. There is no rush; you have done an amazing thing, surviving alone through the mountains for all that time and distance. Praise God, Who has protected and guided you. I am proud of you, my son!"

"Thank you, Uncle. Truly, only God has saved me. There were times when I thought I would not make it. It was a great adventure that taught me what I could not have learned any other way."

We sat quietly for a few more minutes.

"Would you like to take a walk with me in the garden? We can take part in preparing the breakfast."

"I would love that uncle."

I followed him.

"Did you notice the fragrance of these flowers in your room?" pointing to the vine-like shrubs near the building.

"I wouldn't have known, Uncle; I was totally knocked out."

We laughed. A gentle breeze caressed my skin and carried a renewed fragrance through the air that prompted us both to fill our lungs with a deep inhale. The birds' jubilant chirping was coming to a peak in anticipation of the imminent sunrise.

He handed me a flat basket that he grabbed from a nearby table and put a clipping tool in a deep basket that he hung on his arm. strolling along, he selected flowers and gave me each exquisite clipping inquiring "How does this one look?"

I marveled at each, savored the fragrance with joy, and delicately arranged them in the basket to craft a bouquet of nature's finest.

Around the central pool, the graceful arching fruit-laden trees made a colorful reflection in its water against the blue sky. He picked and gave me a few bright orange Persimmons and when he saw me enjoying their fragrance, he remarked, "These trees have borne fruit for years with their heavenly aroma and exquisite taste."

"Shall we venture towards the orchards?" he suggested as we entered a new section with trellises supported on posts that cradled vines above over their horizontal wire mesh. Clusters of grapes dangled above us with a promising bountiful harvest. He spoke as he picked, "Before long, the villagers will gather to reap these grapes, sharing the bounty within the village and beyond."

He picked different fruits along the way and put them in the basket as he talked. I listened carefully and followed him around.

"Plants, my son, epitomize the essence of life through the changing seasons, from the delicate blossoms of spring to the lush growth of summer, the ripe abundance of fall, and the hushed stillness of winter. In this cyclical dance, we bear witness to the unfolding miracles of God, where every moment is purposeful, and nothing occurs by mere chance."

Enveloped in a trance, I felt as though I was traversing through a dream, captivated by every word that fell from my uncle's lips. Amidst this introspection, a realization dawned upon me—I yearned to alleviate my uncle's burdens. His very presence exuded a divine energy that filled me with a sense of completeness and joy. Such emotions were foreign to me, stirring a newfound urgency within me to share my sentiments with him openly. I resolved that he should not bear the weight of my concerns; it was imperative that I express this truth to him with honesty and grace.

We strolled in silence for a brief interlude before I mustered the courage to speak up.

"Uncle, there is a matter of great significance that I wish to share with you," I disclosed earnestly.

Turning towards me, he placed his hand gently on my shoulder, a silent gesture of support as we made our way to a nearby bench. We sat side by side on a curved bench at the periphery of a semicircular garden. The tranquil blend of scents filled the air with the distinct fragrances of Gardenias from one side and roses from the other.

"It brings me immense joy to have you here by my side, my son,"

His words offered a sense of comfort that eased my internal turmoil.

"Thank you, Uncle. I am truly grateful for your kind acceptance of me. I am unable to adequately express my gratitude for your generosity. However, I wish to make it clear, Sir, that I am capable and eager to contribute rather than be a burden to you and your family. Please allow me to lend a helping hand, and feel free to assign me any task that needs attention; if I lack the know-how, I am committed to learning with time. Should you allow me to remain in your care for a while, I am prepared and enthusiastic to fulfill my responsibilities as a humble gesture to contribute towards my upkeep."

His attentive listening was adorned with a gentle smile.

"You, my dear son, are a divine blessing sent to me," he conveyed with sincerity. "Feel free to remain with us for as long as you desire. As the years pass, I find myself in need of assistance, and you, with your youth and willingness, are my perfect choice to uphold my tasks and continue my legacy if you so choose."

I was taken by his generous, humble response. Placing his hand atop mine, he met my gaze directly, and a silent exchange of trust and mutual understanding passed between us.

"You are the one I need by my side more than you need me, my son,"

Overwhelmed by emotion and unable to adequately convey my gratitude through words, I enveloped him in a warm and prolonged embrace as a gesture of my appreciation and love.

"Thank you, Uncle. I am committed to doing everything within my power to assist you in any way possible," I affirmed him with my determined voice to reciprocate his kindness and support.

As we released our embrace, his kind words about my parents, Pari and Sir Farshawd, touched my heart deeply.

"I am certain that Pari and Sir Farshawd hold you close in their hearts and miss you dearly. Let us remember them in our prayers for their well-being..."

Though I longed to hear their names spoken aloud, the ache of missing them weighed heavy on my heart. I hesitated to reveal the depth of my yearning, not to burden him with the sorrow of my longing for my beloved parents.

"Yes, I pray for my father's speedy recovery, Sir. May God Protect and Bliss my parents."

"Amin"

The sunlight filtered through the canopy, casting dramatic, elongated shadows that danced along the ground. Uncle Kia rose from his seat to stretch, retrieving his fruit basket in preparation for departing.

"They must be awake and curious about our whereabouts by now," he remarked with a smile, alluding to the others in the household.

With my basket of bouquets, I followed his leisure stroll back towards the building. The chirping of the birds had subsided with their departure in search of sustenance for the day ahead.

Pausing before the veranda at the top of the stairs, Uncle Kia and I shared a magical moment as we gazed at the azure sky, listened to nature, and savored the scents that filled the air. His presence was peacefully filled with positive energy.

We proceeded to make our way indoors to join the others.

When we arrived at the room where we had enjoyed breakfast together the day before, the table was spread with a variety of food to begin the day with another breakfast.

"Good morning," Uncle Kia announced our arrival in his cheerful tone.

The ladies replied together:

"Good morning... Good morning..."

Banoo was putting the final touches in place as she turned her attention to me with a warm greeting,

"Good morning, Sir Behzawd. I trust you had a

restful night."

"Good morning, Ma'am. Indeed, it was quite rejuvenating. I apologize for my absence throughout yesterday,"

Banoo responded kindly with a reassuring smile, "Oh, please do not worry. Your comfort and well-being are very important. You needed the rest."

With a graceful gesture of her hands, Banoo directed everyone to take their seats, and by what seemed like a curious coincidence, we found ourselves seated in the exact same order as the day before; Banoo sat across the table from Uncle Kia, with me positioned to his right.

Throughout the meal, Uncle Kia and I exchanged occasional glances, each one reaffirming the profound sense of togetherness we shared.

Nadim, attending to the final details of the menu, served the last portions before joining everyone at the table.

Everyone offered me more of this and that out of gracious hospitality. Out of respect and gratitude, I accepted what was offered, even when I felt full and unable to eat. Finally, I had to turn down their offers; "Thank you. I am quite full. Everything is delicious.

Blessed be your offers!"

Uncle Kia looked at Banoo and asked, "Do you need me around, dear?"

"We would love you around, dear, but we should be okay."

Everyone laughed. Then, he stood up and gave a loving pad on Zivar and Negawr's back. Then, he looked at me.

"Do you need more time to rest, my son?"

"Oh, no, Sir. I am all charged up and ready to go."

He smiled, put his hand on my shoulder, and we started to walk out.

The ladies' sendoff made the beginning of the day official:

"God be with you... Blessings... enjoy your day."

We strolled towards the verdant fields. Uncle's spoken words painted a tapestry of ancient wisdom in my mind that defined his profound connection to the land. Each sentence painted the way of life lived by the past generations and was a testament to the enduring legacy of his people.

"The people of this land are masters of their craft,"

he mused in his voice a melody of pride and humility. "From tending the grazing cattle to reaping the bounty of the harvest, we are a symphony of labor and love. I, too, am but a humble note in this grand composition, ever ready to bridge any gap that may arise. Our delivery schedules are meticulously chronicled, a dance of precision to align resources with the population's changing needs."

I found myself lost in the intricate choreography of the village's daily toil. The thought of orchestrating such a harmonious blend of time and manpower filled me with a sense of exhilaration and wonder.

"Tell me, Uncle," I inquired, "do you ever tether your days to the ticking hands of the clock in pursuit of such mastery?"

"No, I trust my men."

"Oh, yes, of course, Sir. I mean, how do you know if the right person is performing the right task? Just trying to understand."

He smiled.

"You know more than you think, my son."

"I hope to learn, Uncle. Thank you for teaching me."

"You can pick anyone to help you get things done. Don't be shy."

"Yes, Sir, thank you, I will."

"Now, let us explore the village together today."

We walked side by side, passing the gardens and entering the open fields. Busy people stopped to greet us, and he introduced me when they came closer to talk.

"Sir Behzawd is my nephew; we are lucky to have him with us …"

"Welcome! Pleased to have you with us, Sir Behzawd. What a great news!"

Some came closer to shake hands with me, and their greetings reflected their sincere acceptance of me as an extended family member. It was the beginning of new friendships with no hesitation.

Chapter 21 A New Sensation

U ncle Kia's every action embodied a graceful homage to the timeless dance of a seeker, moving ever closer to The One, The Beloved, the bestower of sustenance upon all His creation. As I observed his elegant gestures, I couldn't help but sense the profound gravity of his daily physical and spiritual responsibilities weighing heavily upon his weary frame.

Driven by a deep sense of empathy, I endeavored to relieve him of his burdens, delicately coaxing him to share his tasks with me. I offered my solemn vow to attend to them with the utmost care, assuring him that I would nurture them diligently until he felt ready to entrust them entirely to my capable hands.

The tasks entailed the vigilant guardianship of the fields, ensuring the flourishing vitality of the crops, the tender oversight of the stables, where the well-being of the animals was a paramount concern, and the adept management of pressing social affairs as they emerged.

Day by day, Uncle Kia grew more at ease, gradually entrusting me with greater authority over his responsibilities as he learned to rely on my abilities. In doing so, he discovered a newfound liberation from the physical burdens that had weighed him down for as long as he could remember. Despite his diminishing involvement, his spirit persisted in intermittent visits, always departing with kind words of encouragement and praise.

In Sawmawn, I bloomed. Intertwined within the complex tapestry of the villagers' lives, I was embraced into their inner sanctums as I partook in their sorrows and joys.

The highlight of my day unfolded in the serene confines of Uncle's library, a haven of wisdom and solace. Here, I would meet with him once my toil had subsided, just before joining the familial gathering for supper. Enveloped by his vast collection of volumes of books that encompassed agricultural techniques, medical wisdom, and philosophical ponderings to the celestial ballet of astrology, I found myself spellbound until the call to dine beckoned us. Uncle, a luminary of erudition, possessed a profound comprehension of each tome that graced his shelves. He bestowed wisdom upon me, enlightening my mind with every question that arose as we navigated through the challenging pages together.

Like a nurturing mentor, Uncle not only attended to my inquiries but also kindled a desire within me to delve deeper into the diverse reservoirs of knowledge that nourished the foundations of my understanding. Through our heartfelt dialogues, we exchanged perspectives on a myriad of topics, akin to flexing my mental muscles to facilitate further growth and understanding.

A deeper spiritual connection was also evolving through our meditative pauses at the beginning and end of each day. During these moments, he led me in a gentle chorus of prayers, enveloping us in a serene atmosphere as the world around us settled into a tranquil hush.

Two years drifted by before I discerned a subtle weariness of enigmatic emotions seeping into my world that I hesitated to confront within the recesses of my mind. Despite finding solace in the fulfilling labor of my tasks and the intellectual journeys with Uncle, a quiet restlessness tugged at my heartstrings, urging me to return to the place where Negawr's presence transformed ordinary walls into a sanctuary of serenity and tranquility.

Although she was two years my junior, she possessed a myriad of exceptional qualities that evoked memories of my mother. Her large amber-brown eyes carried a depth capable of peering directly into my soul with a single glance. She exuded wisdom, maturity, creativity, and intelligence with a touch of divine mystique. Her tender kindness and unwavering courage made her a truly remarkable individual.

With profound reverence, I hesitated to fully acknowledge my emotions, even to myself. The mere act of breathing the same air as she felt like a stroke of serendipity, joyfully reshaping my world into a life that seemed inconceivable without her presence. In waking hours, I longed to be in her presence, and in slumber, she danced graceful melodies of life in the tapestries of my dreams.

"Oh, Lord, The Most Gracious One, thank You. You create perfection, indeed. Could it be in Your plans for me to be by her side for life?"

Upon reflection, I discerned the delicate threads of affection beginning to weave themselves from the very first moments we met at the gate. Her graceful movements, akin to a feather dancing in the wind, exuded vitality through her natural beauty and innate modesty.

In the face of the irresistible allure that drew me towards her, I exerted a conscious effort to quell the thoughts and emotions taking root within me. Yet, with each passing moment, it became increasingly clear that my feelings transcended beyond our kinship or the deep respect and admiration I had for her. Even the brief period of her absence during the fleeting moments of her solitary daily pilgrimage to fetch water from the spring draped a haunting veil of melancholy over my heart.

Her journey to the spring unfolded as an elegant narrative in its own right. Her whispered expressions of gratitude and reverence against the background natural symphony that enveloped the surroundings offered praises to the Ever-Present One. With each step along her path, the large clay pitcher perched gracefully upon her shoulder, brimming with water as she made her return, resembled a sacred offering in a divine dance.

"I must discuss my emotions with Uncle Kia," I reiterated to myself with the growing tug in my heart, all the while knowing that engaging in private conversations with her was not an honorable course of action.

Three years flew by in Sawmawn. By societal norms, I had reached the age when marriage was deemed appropriate.

"Negawr is my chosen partner for life, the only one; she is the one I love and cherish… Marriage, indeed, is the only path for me to stand by her side."

Chapter 22 The Question

I t had been a while since I commenced my mornings with visiting the spring after the prayer. There, atop a weathered boulder, I gazed out at the breathtaking panorama spread before me. Always accompanied by the melodic trill of birds and the soft murmur of the river as I sought solace and divine inspiration before embarking on the day's labor ahead.

"Would it be deemed honorable to solicit Negawr's guidance prior to engaging in conversation with Uncle Kia?" was the inquiry weighing on my mind, as I harbored no desire to act in opposition to her wishes. "Does she even consider me as a suitable life companion?"

The sky blazed with hues of orange and red before sunrise. Lost in contemplation of the intricate dance of patterns, shapes, and the swift passage of billowing clouds, I was suddenly jolted from my reverie by an unexpected greeting.

'Peace and Blessings, Sir Behzawd."

I panicked with a hasty rise to my feet as Negawr set down the large clay pitcher from her shoulder.

A torrent of uncertainty flooded my mind. "had she

caught wind of my innermost thoughts, or had she perhaps mistaken them for a melody escaping my lips?"

"Peace and Blessings to you as well, Miss Negawr. What a beautiful morning."

"I love mornings. They exude beauty and purity."

"Indeed, may I help? Allow me to fill it up for you?"

as I pointed to the pitcher.

Interpreting her graceful smile as tacit approval, I filled the pitcher with water as she stood there bashful, observing my actions. I grappled with the decision of whether to voice my question as I placed the pitcher before her with a lowered gaze fixed upon the pitcher.

"The water is delightfully cold," I remarked, though it was a trivial observation borne out of my uncertainty about where to begin.

"Yes, indeed. Cold and fresh, the perpetual flow patiently awaits appreciation," she replied with a serene demeanor.

"Perpetual, Infinite blessings, blessings beyond measure, indeed," I echoed softly.

A moment of silence enveloped us before I gently

broke it.

"Miss Negawr, would you care to have a seat for a few moments?" I inquired, gesturing towards a nearby rock just a few feet from my earlier perch.

I retreated a few paces back to my own spot as she settled. Our momentary silence was filled with the tranquil sounds of water and nature.

Struggling to grasp my elusive words.

"Miss Negawr, I have pondered this for some time..." I paused, letting the gravity of my words linger in the air while she gazed at me expectantly. "I have a question, but I am not sure how to begin." I paused to gather my thoughts. "Would you permit me... would you mind if I sought your father's blessing for your hand in marriage?"

The words escaped my lips, carrying with them a weight that seemed to fill the air.

She blushed, her cheeks tinted with a rosy hue. Her eyes lingered on the flowing water before meeting mine with a bashful smile. Gazed at the flowing water, then met my eyes with a bashful smile. I detected a subtle nod of approval, prompting me to await her response with bated breath.

She rose to her feet. "I must return. Breakfast must

be ready by now."

Her soft yet decisive words marked the conclusion of our shared moment by the river's edge, allowing unspoken emotions to linger between us like ripples on the surface of the stream. A sense of suspense and fear gripped me.

"I sincerely apologize," I began, my voice tinged with regret. "I did not mean any disrespect. Please forgive me." With a genuine sense of remorse, I awaited her reaction.

Our eyes met in a fleeting glance.

"We must wait to see what Father will say," she spoke softly, her words carrying a weight of anticipation like a veil of suspense.

She gracefully lifted the pitcher and balanced it on her head with the poise of a ballerina.

"Thank you for your help," she said with a warm and appreciative voice. "Shall we make our way back for breakfast?" Her words, akin to a delicate dance of unspoken sentiments, gently guided us back to the routine amidst the swirling emotions that lingered between us.

As she began to walk, I followed closely behind, eager to keep her company and perhaps hear more.

"Is it alright if I speak with Uncle Kia about us?" I asked tentatively, like a whispered secret.

She turned to me; her lips traced a delicately preserved smile. The meeting of our eyes conveyed a silent assurance before she resumed her walk. My knees trembled beneath me with the weight of the moment.

"If you don't mind, I would like to stay here for a few more minutes, but I will join you for breakfast shortly," I said to gain a moment of respite that I felt engulfed with.

Like a ballerina executing a half turn, she glanced back at me and waved her hand in a gesture of graceful understanding before resuming her walk. I stood there on trembling knees and watched her recede into the distance.

Once I was certain that she would not turn back, I sank down onto the ground, my eyes fixed on her retreating figure as she moved away. The vibrant hues of her long, flowing dress lent a touch of drama to her graceful stride, painting a picture of elegance in motion. Her last lingering gaze and warm smile ignited a newfound determination within me, propelling me forward with strengthened resolve for the next step.

For days, I found myself imagining scenarios as I

mentally prepared myself for a special meeting with Uncle Kia.

"I must request a special meeting with Uncle," I deliberated in my self-reflecting thoughts. "Would he deem me worthy of his daughter's trust? Can he place his trust in me?" I pondered, consumed by the weight of similar questions, as I envisioned the pivotal encounter that lay ahead.

"I must request a special meeting with Uncle."

One evening, on my late return from the fields, I encountered Uncle in the garden.

"Greetings, Uncle," I greeted him with reverence.

"Greetings to you, my son. How was your day? It seems you have had a long day,"

"Full of Blessings, praise God. How are you, my beloved Uncle?" I replied gratefully, acknowledging the grace in my day.

"I see you have crafted another beautiful bouquet. Allow me to guess... Is it for Lady Banoo?" I inquired. We laughed, recognizing Uncle Kia's penchant for creating floral gifts for his beloved Lady Banoo.

As we ascended the stairs together, he placed a comforting hand on my shoulder as he spoke. This silent gesture was his normal way of camaraderie and support that energized me with confidence.

"When I pick flowers, my son, I think of everybody, but of course, I hope Lady Banoo would like them too."

"You have an exquisite touch, Uncle. I am sure she loves your flowers."

Laughter filled the air as we reached the top of the stairs. Uncle Kia, as was his custom, paused on the veranda, his gaze turning towards the sky. The orange-red hues of the sunset painted a breathtaking tableau before us, reminiscent of a masterful painting. In the tranquil moment that followed, we stood in companionable silence, gazing at the ever-changing canvas of the sky. As the first star made its appearance, a sense of calm washed over me, emboldening me to speak.

"Uncle Kia, there is an important matter I wish to discuss with you," I ventured, my voice steady despite the weight of uncertainty that lingered in the evening air.

We giggled. Once at the top of the stairs, he paused in the veranda, as he usually did, and looked at the sky. The orange-red sunset was awe inspiring, like a brilliant painting. We stood there in silence, watching for a while. With the sighting of the first star, my fears disappeared, and I found the courage to ask.

"Uncle Kia, I need to talk about something important with you."

"Sure, my son. Now?" he inquired with his reassuring, gentle voice.

"No, it can wait."

"How about the day after tomorrow? Friday, we can spend some time in the garden together before supper." He suggested with his usual warmth and understanding.

"Yes, Sir, Friday in the garden would be wonderful. Thank you," I responded with gratitude and anticipation.

Uncle placed his hand on my shoulder for reassurance. Together, we stepped inside to the comforting embrace of the family supper. Amidst the chatter and laughter, my mind lingered on the memory of my encounter with Negawr at by the spring and the possibilities ahead. Despite the subtle allure emanating from her mere presence, I deliberated in avoiding her gaze.

Chapter 23 The Request

Fridays were cherished family moments and joyous social gatherings, interwoven with moments of leisure and reflection. The midafternoon bathing served as a catalyst for organizing my thoughts. As the sun began its descent, I eagerly slipped into the exquisite attire procured from the venerable tailor's shop in town, each stitch whispering tales of craftsmanship and elegance.

While my mother had always curated our formal wardrobes with her impeccable taste, this was the first tailored attire that I, as a grown man, selected myself since my arrival in Sawmawn.

This handpicked ensemble was crafted from a soft white fabric reminiscent of a kimono, cascading almost to the floor. As I secured the marine-blue belt adorned with intricate white embroidery, the garment barely skimmed my ankles. Layered on top, a marine-blue vest embellished along its open front descended to my knees as a formal outfit.

As the time neared five o'clock, I strolled towards our usual alcove within the garden, contemplating every word I needed to say. The blue sky reflected a deep blue opening amidst its billowing white clouds in the central pool, creating an ethereal spectacle that blurred the boundaries between heaven and earth.

"I wonder if that means something about my enquiry," I pondered as I caught sight of Uncle Kia approaching. Walking over, I greeted him and pressed a tender kiss to his hand once I reached him. A radiant smile illuminated his face with a playful compliment.

"My son, you look splendid! Am I honored to join you somewhere?"

His words elicited shared laughter, a familiar melody of camaraderie between us. With his gentle hand on my back, we made our way to our favorite nook and nestled amidst fragrant flowers. This intimate alcove had borne witness to many of our shared memories and contemplative conversations over time.

After our initial greetings, I had a sense that he might already know why we were there. Breaking a momentary silence, I said, "Dearest Uncle, I am truly grateful for what you have done for me."

Before I could continue, he interrupted, "Oh, no, that's what I say to you, my son. I am practically retired because you have undertaken all my strenuous tasks."

"You are most kind, Uncle. I am simply fulfilling my duty, and I wish I could do more."

"I want you to know that I am very pleased with you. I hope you are satisfied with your life here."

"Oh, yes, Uncle, I could not have asked for more. Everything is perfect, and I am learning to do better."

"I am glad, my son."

"Dear Uncle, I need to ask you about something very important to me."

"Anything, my son. You can be frank with me."

I composed my words with a pause.

"Would you consider me worthy of being your son-in-law?"

"Oh, yes, of course. You are just the right man, the perfect son-in-law I have always hoped for, congratulations."

What a relief. With a renewed confidence, I continued, "Thank you, Uncle. Would you entrust me with Miss Negawr's hand in marriage?"

He became quiet, shifted in his seat, leaned back slightly, and took a deep breath. A faded smile altered his jolly expression.

"My son, the cultural norm in Sawmawn is that a younger sibling cannot get married before their elder."

My heart sank.

"You will have to wait until Miss Zivar is married first."

I had never thought much about cultural boundaries and limitations. In processing his response and evaluating my hope, I sat quietly, unable to move, overwhelmed with a sense of grief. Then, I heard Uncle calling my name.

"Behzawd, my son, are you okay? Behzawd."

Snaping out of my shattered dream, I found my head on his chest as he called my name.

"Behzawd,"

Panicked and worried, he tapped on my face and shoulder. I forced myself up to sit straight.

"Oh, sorry, Sir."

I wanted to cry, but that didn't feel manly. I gripped the edge of the bench tightly, swallowed the lump in my throat, and squeezed my burning eyes.

"Yes, Sir, I am okay."

Chapter 24 Proposition

The first thing I noticed after I don't remember how long, was the shifting clouds reflected in the pool. The peculiar hole had vanished. I was oblivious to my surroundings and the passage of time until Uncle's voice broke through some kind of stillness, pulling me back into the present.

Initially, he sounded distant and indistinct, like faint whispers in the wind. Gradually, as Uncle's voice gained clarity, a particular phrase pierced through the haze, snapping me out of my reverie that brought me back to a heightened awareness of the current reality.

"My son, I have a solution. Would you care to hear?" his voice filled with anticipation.

"a solution?" I felt nauseous. The only thought echoing in my mind was, "I cannot marry Negawr. What solution is there?"

I pondered silently, convinced that nothing could ease my anguish.

Undeterred, he continued, "You can Marry Zivar,"

I leaped from my seat in a reflexive jolt.

"I respect Miss Zivar as a sister. We are of the same

age. She deserves someone of greater maturity than I. Please forgive me, Uncle, but my heart belongs to Miss Negawr."

Unconvinced, he persisted, "Being of the same age might indeed prove advantageous, my son. It is likely to foster deep understanding between partners, paving the way for a harmonious life."

Numb, nauseated, and utterly depleted of energy, I found myself incapable of engaging in such a preposterous proposition. The concept seemed entirely misguided.

"You need not rush into a decision, dear. Take your time. For nearly four years, I have been blessed with the most fulfilling moments of my life with you, akin to the son I never had. You are my most trusted confidant. Exercise patience; either wait until Zivar finds a suitable partner or take the initiative to bring your union with Negawr to fruition."

Suddenly, a glimmer of hope ignited within me. I was prepared to go to any lengths to turn that dream into reality.

"I am willing to do anything, Uncle, but how can that be?" I inquired eagerly.

"I am wary of entrusting my daughters' futures to

just anyone. It is not clear when a suitable suitor will emerge whom I can approve for Zivar. However, I would have no reservations if you were to seek her hand in marriage," he expressed candidly.

"I am truly honored, Uncle, but my heart belongs to Miss Negawr. How could I entertain the thought of marrying Miss Zivar?" I expressed with sincerity.

"Yes, my son, I understand. Then, you must wait until there is a match for Zivar," he acknowledged.

Feeling a mix of sickness and bewilderment, I grappled with the weight of the situation.

"But if you were to wed Zivar and remained in my service for a total of ten years since your arrival here, you would then have my wholehearted blessing to marry Negawr," he proposed.

I gazed at him in silence, a mixture of disbelief and revulsion stirring within me.

"In terms of logistics, my son, you have amassed ample resources to cover Zivar's dowry. Should you consent to the ten-year arrangement, you will have also fulfilled the requirements for Negawr's dowry. In this way, all will be sanctified, and your desires may come to fruition, God willing," he rationalized.

Overwhelmed by the unpleasant and tense nature

of the discussion, my stomach churning and heart aching, I contemplated excusing myself from the conversation.

"I am not feeling well. Please excuse me," I murmured softly.

"Let's head inside so you can lie down," he suggested, his tone filled with concern.

Summoning all my strength, I pushed myself up to stand on my feet. He rose to assist me, offering support by holding my arm.

"Thank you, Uncle. I need to take a walk," in my strained voice.

"Would you like me to accompany you?" he inquired with evident concern.

"Be careful, my son. God be with you," he wished me.

Feeling off-balance on shaky legs, I clutched at branches, tree trunks, the edges of tables—anything within reach—to steady myself and avert a fall.

"Oh, Lord, please save me in Your Grace, guide me to walk in Your path, the path of those upon whom You have bestowed Your Grace..." I whispered prayers as I dragged my feet toward the nearest gate, nauseated and dizzy.

Uncle's words pounded in my head. Aimless and devoid of desire to see or speak with anyone, I retreated into solitude.

Chapter 25 New Reality

By night fall, weary from wandering aimlessly through the woods beyond the open fields, I settled upon a solitary rock. The deep blue expanse above me unveiled a spectacle of twinkling stars one at a time. Was it possible that my own celestial companion resided among them, dancing alongside Negawr's?

The notion of wedlock with another fair maiden seemed preposterous, for my heart was already irrevocably entwined with Negawr's.

In my heart, the path to union with Negawr seemed elusive, dependent upon the arrival of a worthy suitor for Zivar or the unlikely event of my marriage to her, followed by a patient vigil spanning seven long years.

Neither prospect offered a comforting solace for prolonged contemplation. Exhausted, I reclined on my back and swiftly yielded to sleep. The melodic chirping of birds woke me up at dawn.

I must make my way to the spring to meet with Negawr and relay Uncle's response. I thought, even if she does not come, I will still wash and offer my prayers at that sacred place before heading to the fields.

The cold water was rejuvenating to my weary soul. The flowing waters echoed the whispers of my prayers that enveloped me in serenity.

"Oh, Creator of the heavens and earth, bless our journey with Your Divine Wisdom, illuminate us with Your Guiding Light. Lord, I am grateful for Your divine plan, though I know not, guide me, Your humble servant, forgive my transgressions, You alone are All-Knowing, All-Merciful, grant me the strength to keep my heart open, by Your grace …"

As I pondered the transformed atmosphere of our meeting place since my last encounter with Negawr, a sense of melancholy tugged at my heart. At sunrise, while preparing to depart, I caught sight of Negawr approaching with a pitcher gracefully balanced atop her head. Overwhelmed with anticipation, I quickly brushed off the dust from the clothing I had worn since the day before and hurried to meet her.

"Good morning, Miss Negawr,"

"Good morning, Sir Behzawd. How are you? Father was worried about you; he mentioned that you were unwell yesterday. You did not return home last night."

"I apologize. I am quite perplexed by the cultural norms here. Were you aware of the tradition that Miss

Zivar must marry first?"

"Yes, I was aware," Negawr responded calmly, "but there is no need for you to be so distraught. It is not the end of the world."

"How long do you reckon it would take for a suitable man to arrive and from where to gain Uncle's approval?" I asked in confusion.

After a thoughtful pause, she responded, "I understand your concerns. Consider this: perhaps Zivar would be a more suitable companion for you than I am. Plus, despite the length of time it may require, remember, where there's a will, there's a way."

"But we are discussing a lifelong commitment, dear Miss Negawr," I expressed with uncertainty.

"This could indeed be a test for all involved, Sr. Behzawd," her tone of voice conveying her acceptance of the potential outcome.

We made our way to the spring, where she carefully set the pitcher beside her as we settled on our spots. The birds' chirping added the final touch to the peaceful flowing water for a perfect symphony of nature.

"We must put our present on hold for an indefinite period of time," I said with a weight of uncertainty.

Negawr slipped off her slippers and dipped her feet into the water, a gesture that seemed to invite a cleansing of our minds and a release of our burdens. Following her lead, I, too, immersed my feet in the ice-cold water. A shiver ran down my spine as I contemplated.

"Our worlds are connected by this pristine water," I mused, acknowledging the symbolic bond that flowed between us in that moment of shared tranquility.

I stole a quick glance at her and noticed a struggle in her eyes.

"Oh, God, my intention was to bring her joy, yet I have only brought her sorrow. Please lead our hearts according to Your divine will," I silently prayed.

Her emotional gaze was heavy to bear.

"Seven years will pass in the blink of an eye, Sir Behzawd. It is but a fleeting moment in the grand scheme of things," Negawr reassured me with a gentle tone, offering me a glimmer of hope amidst the uncertainty that enveloped us.

"Are you suggesting that you approve of my marrying another woman?"

"Everything in this world happens with purpose,"

Negawr articulated, emphasizing each word with precision. "Our existence in this earthly realm is a brief interlude, a mere bridge to a vast eternity. The challenges we face in this realm serve as catalysts for growth, propelling us towards higher planes within the eternal sphere. Our ascension is only made possible only when we submit our own will to the Divine Will."

"But this unjust decree is a cultural norm, not a divine decree."

"Indeed, the majority of ingrained wisdom within these cultural norms is essential for transcending our individual selves through our embracing, yielding, and adhering to adversities."

Overwhelmed and embarrassed by my selfish reflections, I was compelled to admire her selfless outlook on life.

"My dear Miss Negawr, seven years encompass a significant span of time, ripe with possibilities and transformations. It seems only fair that you, too, should have the liberty to marry a deserving suitor of your choice should I decide to wed Miss Zivar."

The sun was well up in the sky, casting long, early morning shadows to the west. Our feet, cold and washed clean, bounded our silent promise by the water.

As she slipped on her sandals and rose to depart, I swiftly refilled the pitcher and placed it before her.

"Thank you, Sir. Behzawd."

"You are most welcome, my dear Miss Negawr," I responded, aching to offer her the world.

She balanced the pitcher atop her head with a gentle smile adorning her face that imbued our parting with a sense of solemn grace. She started her walk home. I trailed behind, longing for a few more paces.

Then, I stopped and let her go. A silent farewell lingered in the air as I watched her continue on her way.

Chapter 26 Marriage Ceremony

Uncle Kia's expectations for his prospective sons-in-law bore the weight of faith and lineage. As I fervently prayed and yearned for the best qualified suitor to enter Zivar's life, my heart ached with anticipation.

"Oh, Lord, illuminate my path, for Negawr is my chosen companion, my only soulmate, is she not? Grant me the vision to perceive as You Wish, my Lord, and lead me to the straight path."

Each night, I clung to the hope of awakening from the torment of this nightmare and returning to a semblance of normal life. I sought solace amidst sorrow by pouring my heart into prayers and toil. Conversations held little appeal, even with Uncle Kia, yet our exchanges remained respectful and warm. He understood the weight of my burden and honored the solitude I sought for my grieving heart.

"Lord, You are my shepherd. I was lost and knew nothing when You guided me without my asking. I am but a timid sheep, prone to stray without Your steadfast guidance. With an open heart, I embrace Your Will and renounce the clamor of my desires. Lead me along the path of Truth, that I may serve You faithfully."

To truly be His sheep, I had to cultivate a deeper trust in His guidance to aquire unwavering faith in the One Who Knows, Sees, and Hears all.

As months drifted by, I found solace in the busyness of my daily tasks, steering clear of any situations that might lead to discussions on delicate matters. I noticed Uncle Kia sitting alone in our cherished spot in the garden on a Friday. A pang of regret tugged at my heart for having neglected our time together for so long.

"Hello, Uncle, I see you are by yourself. May I keep you company?"

"Hello, my son, of course. It would bring me great joy if you did."

"How are you, Uncle?"

"Praise God, I am well, thank you, my son. And how have you been?"

"Praise God, I am doing alright. Please forgive me, Uncle. I have missed our time together."

"I understand, son. It takes time to navigate the complexities of adulthood."

"It is agonizing to wait without knowing for how long."

"Yes, my son, especially when we fixate on one dream."

"But what if that dream is the only dream?"

"How can you discover what other dreams may unfold if you focus on one? Sometimes, we must venture into the unknown with courage."

"And how does that relate to my situation, Uncle?"

"In your particular situation, my suggestion would be to marry Zivar, as it could help bring clarity to some of your uncertainties and pave the way for your short and long-term goals."

"Even if those goals may not necessarily align with my dreams? With all due respect, Uncle, it seems your proposal is more in line with your own aspirations."

"And yours, my son. Is building your own family not a goal of yours?"

"I suppose that's one perspective."

"Well, you are free to do so whenever you desire, my son. Since we do not know when Zivar will accept a qualified suiter to marry, you have my blessings to marry someone of your own choice other than Negawr."

"My dearest Uncle, I hold Miss Zivar in the highest

regard, but my heart is with Miss Negawar."

"I understand, my son. Perhaps it would be wise to wait for a suitable individual to arrive, one whom Zivar will accept."

"And therein lies the uncertainty: the unsettling doubt of when, or if, that fateful hope will ever come to fruition."

"Indeed, my son. My offer remains open, awaiting your nod to embark on the journey of starting your own family. Should you opt to join hands with Zivar, the serene eastern quarter of this compound may serve as a perfect haven for embracing your burgeoning family. As you ponder the future, envision crafting your second sanctuary in the northern quarter, a prelude to your impending union with Negawr, in celebration of the tenth anniversary of your time in Sawmawn."

"You make it sound so easy, Uncle."

"My son, life is not as complicated as we think."

"If we were to proceed with your proposal, Miss Negawr would be free to marry a man of her choice should such a suitor cross her path in the interim. Would that be just and fair?"

"You possess wisdom beyond your years, my son. I trust your judgment, and we shall reach that decision collectively should such a man present himself."

"Thank you, Uncle. I have strong faith in your judgment. Please allow me to take my time as I ponder over this."

"Would you mind if I seek my daughter's perspective on this matter?"

"By all means, this decision pertains to Miss Zivar more than anyone else."

"May you find happiness, my son, by the Grace of God."

Three days later, during a family gathering, Banoo shared the news.

"… We are delighted to announce our beloved Zivar and Sr. Behzawd soon to be united in matrimony. We have much to celebrate …"

I watched everyone, including Negawr, be genuinely happy for her sister while I buried something dep within my heart alone.

Preparations were swiftly underway. The entire village rejoiced in our wedding festivities within a mere two weeks. Negawr stood by Zivar's side as her steadfast confidante throughout the ceremony. Banoo orchestrated the arrangements for the celebrations with the assistance of her committed village volunteers.

The two weeks' time was also a busy time in the eastern quarter with renovations and preparations. On the eve of our wedding, Banoo and Uncle Kia hosted a housewarming gathering there, inviting Zivar and me, along with a select group of family members, including Negawr. The residence exuded comfort, with its interior predominantly adorned by handmade articles that Zivar and Negawr had made.

Following a tour of the premises, Uncle and I strolled out together. Ensuring privacy, Uncle whispered in my ear, making sure no one else could overhear, "My son, this is our gift to you and Zivar. We hope that it brings you both happiness and prosperity in comfort."

"Thank you, Uncle. Your generosity exceeds my expectations. This was truly unnecessary; I am deeply grateful."

"I am simply doing what any loving uncle would do, my son, plus, who knows, it may allow me to enjoy the blessings of having grandchildren sooner while I am here."

"Thank you, Sir. I wish you a long and healthy life for another hundred years."

"Oh, hoo, hoo," he chuckled, "I don't think I have much time left, my son. It brings me comfort to know you are here to carry on in my stead."

"I could never replace you, Sir. I rely on your guidance and presence by my side."

We continued our conversation on our journey home, following his favorite path through the gardens.

The following day, the wedding and festivities unfolded as scheduled. The marriage ceremony was held inside Uncle's reception hall, followed by joyful celebrations in its front garden.

Close to midnight, Uncle Kia stepped forward, extending a hand to clasp mine on one side and Zivar's on the other.

"My beloved ones, I am grateful for each of you for being at the heart of this celebration," he expressed before turning to face the guests, "Let us now escort our blessed bride and groom to their new home."

Banoo and Negawr, draped in flowing white garments, walked gracefully on either side of Zivar, who was adorned in a vibrant, colorful dress complemented by a semi-transparent veil delicately veiling her head and face. The guests enveloped the trio, their voices merging in harmonious melodies of well-wishes and happy songs. Approaching the newly renovated edifice in the eastern quarter, the onlookers hurriedly arranged themselves into two parallel lines along the pathway adorned with an array of colorful blooms.

Standing resolutely ahead of the assembled guests, Uncle and I awaited the approaching trio at the entrance. As they approached, Uncle gently placed Zivar's hand in mine, his voice trembling with emotion as he imparted his heartfelt blessings,

"The future is yours. May your home be blessed."

With a gentle gesture, he stepped aside, granting us passage into the abode. Banoo, Uncle, and Negawr followed suit, forming a solemn procession into the dwelling. A chorus of cheers, well-wishes, and applause erupted from the guests—a jubilant celebration of our entry into our new home.

Zivar and I led our small group of five along the remaining flower-lined pathway, ascending the stairs that led to the veranda of our new home. Pausing at the top, we turned and waved gratefully to our guests. Banoo and Uncle enveloped us in warm embraces with love and pride. Negawr shared a tender moment with her sister, exchanging a heartfelt kiss before departing. Bidding a final good night, they joined the other guests, disappearing into the night within moments.

Zivar and I stood in quiet contemplation, gazing up at the twinkling stars above us. Breaking the silence, I addressed her gently, "You must be weary, dear Miss Zivar. Would you like to retire inside?" Uncertain of an appropriate address.

"Thank you, dear Behzawd; you must be exhausted as well," she responded.

"You've shouldered much over these past days, and today was truly special. I am grateful," I expressed, attempting to bridge the gap and create a more comfortable, informal atmosphere between us.

"Yes, my beloved Behzawd, today was indeed a beautiful day, perhaps the finest of my life," Zivar replied warmly.

"Praise be to God," I whispered as we entered our shared abode, stepping forward together into this new chapter of our lives.

As the days passed, our bond deepened, and I found myself inevitably falling in love with this remarkable, compassionate, and utterly selfless woman who was now my wife. Zivar's unwavering kindness and dedication never ceased to astound me.

"You anticipate my needs before I even realize them, Zivar," I confessed, filled with admiration and humility in the face of her innate thoughtfulness. Her gracious nature often left me feeling overwhelmed with a sense of unworthiness.

Despite being showered with love and care beyond measure, a pang of guilt would intermittently tug at my heart, serving as a poignant reminder of the shadow of neglect that loomed over Negawr. Our interactions gradually grew sparse as I consciously suppressed any emotions that might jeopardize my unwavering commitment to Zivar. Above all, motivated by a deep-rooted sense of respect, my primary aspiration was to grant Negawr the freedom to release herself from any perceived obligation towards me.

I began to forgo my visits to the spring and headed straight home after a taxing day's work to share dinner with Zivar.

Meanwhile, Negawr quietly tended to her own life, finding solace in the comforting presence of her parents.

In the midst of our evolving family dynamic, Zivar welcomed our first son, Puyaw, before our first wedding anniversary. Subsequently, our second son, Armin, arrived in the second year of our marriage, followed by the birth of our next four sons in each consecutive year that followed.

Negawr wholeheartedly embraced each new addition to our family with genuine joy. Collaborating with nannies, she lovingly cared for the children as if they were her own, and her happiness was mirrored in the laughter and playfulness she shared with them and Zivar. The bond between the two sisters continued its resilience, perfectly aligned with their respective natures. In an effort to give the sisterly space they needed; I kept myself occupied with my increasing tasks to allow Uncle to retire.

"Oh, Lord, please bless Negawr with abundant happiness. If it is Your divine will, may she find a deserving partner who can provide her with both prosperity and genuine joy." I kept Negawr in my prayers.

Negawr's days were filled with meaningful pursuits that kept her busy and content. In addition to caring for her parents, supporting Zivar and our children, and offering aid to those in need, she seized any spare moment to expand her knowledge and skills. Her innate positivity illuminated the world around her, leaving a trail of warmth and light wherever she went.

Year after year, eligible suitors from both near and far came forward to seek Negawr's hand in marriage. In a thoughtful and cautious manner, Uncle entrusted me with the task of thoroughly vetting each potential match before seeking Negawr's opinion. Those who successfully cleared the background check underwent Uncle's careful consideration and discussion with Negawr herself.

Despite the presence of several highly qualified suitors, Negawr remained resolute in her decision-making, consistently turning down even the most promising of proposals. Her reasons, though diverse, consistently underscored her discerning nature and the importance she placed on finding a truly compatible match.

Chapter 27 Last Wish

Zivar embraced every fleeting moment of life with an open heart, dedicating herself tirelessly to the needs of our expanding family. However, nearly seven years into our marriage, as we awaited the arrival of our sixth child, a specter of illness descended upon her, casting a dark shadow over the entire family.

Multiple medical experts kept a vigilant watch over her deteriorating condition around the clock. The arrival of the new baby brought a sense of relief, easing the immediate danger to both mother and child. Hopeful prayers for Zivar's swift recovery echoed throughout the village. As weeks turned into a blur of uncertainty, the medical team continued to wrestle with the enigmatic puzzle of her declining health, with each passing moment shrouded in mounting concern.

Beset by labored breathing and unexplained, excruciating pains in her chest and abdomen, even the most basic movements became a torment for Zivar. Every breath was a battle against an unseen, merciless adversary, leaving everyone around her consumed by deep-seated worry and helplessness.

My time at home was spent primarily at Zivar's

bedside, with brief departures only for essential tasks. One early morning, as a few others tended to her in the room and exhaustion claimed her, she drifted off to sleep. Reluctant to attend to an urgent matter of business, I stepped away. Suddenly, I was hastily summoned back upon learning that she had requested my presence.

Rushing to her side, I found her still, her eyes closed in peaceful repose. The tranquil stillness that transformed her delicate form in a matter of minutes struck me deeply. Seated beside her, I gently clasped her hand in mine in silent acknowledgment of our bond.

"Hello, my sweet Zivar, I am here," I whispered softly. With a determined effort, she slowly opened her eyes, striving to maintain her gaze on me.

"Behzawd, my dearest one, could we have a moment alone, please?" Her voice, though faint, carried a weight of longing and urgency.

With a courteous nod, I motioned for everyone to leave, allowing us the privacy she sought in a poignant moment.

"We are alone, my dear,"

Her fragile whisper was barely audible in the quiet

room.

"I … I need …"

"I am listening to you, sweetheart," my heart aching to ease her agony.

"I need you to promise me something," she urged, her eyes searching mine for assurance. "I won't be here much longer."

"No, no, my darling, you must rest now; you will gain your strength back soon," I interjected with a heartfelt hope.

She shook her head gently, a wistful smile tugging at the corner of her lips. "No, my sweet Behzawd. I am aware that my time has come."

She was certain her time on this earth was coming to an end, and my words could not sway her conviction.

"My dearest Zivar, you must fight to get well, for me, for our children, for us," I pleaded desperately.

"Please … my love … my beloved Behzawd, hear me now. I am profoundly grateful for the blessings we have shared. With you by my side, every moment has been a treasure, making me feel like the luckiest woman in the whole world. But now, as fate calls me to depart this life, I implore you to make me a sacred vow," her words trembled with each labored breath.

"Anything you ask, my dearest," I whispered.

"Please promise me that you will marry Beeta, my trusted maid. She has been a nurturing presence to our children... they adore her... and you will need assistance in raising them,"

"I can manage everything until you recover, my love. Do not worry,"

"Please, my dear Behzawd, give me your word."

"Alright, my dear, I promise, but I want you here. We need you, my sweetheart," I whispered in a bid to uphold her fading strength. It was the meager comfort I could offer amidst her torment as she teetered on what she believed to be her last moments.

She took a deep breath, mustering all her strength to squeeze my hand in gratitude. A faint smile graced her lips as a serene expression of contentment settled on her face. Then, her grip loosened.

"Zivar, oh, my love, Zivar"

Her soul had departed. "Doctor!" I called out in desperation, but he could not revive her.

A profound silence descended upon the world,

casting a shadow over every member of our family and the village with heavy weight. It was a struggle to accept her absence. Yet, as certain as the passage of life itself, she had embraced death before my eyes.

Zivar's death left a profound void that was difficult to fill by one or two people. She embodied a selfless, kind soul whom I had grown to cherish deeply aside from being the devoted mother of our children.

To honor my promise to Zivar, I sought a private conversation with Beeta after several months had passed.

"Miss Beeta, I am immensely grateful for all that you have done. Laldy Zivar entrusted you with the care of our children from the very beginning of their lives. Her last wish was for me to marry you. Would you be willing to stand by my side as my wife and nurture our children?"

She blushed and replied, "Oh, Sir Behzawd, I would be deeply honored, Sir. Your children are as dear to me as if they were my own. May God bless Lady Zivar's soul."

In a private ceremony, we exchanged vows and became husband and wife. Following our marriage, Beeta moved into Zivar's room.

Chapter 28 Awaited Time

The family was shattered by the loss of Zivar. Uncle Kia and Banoo were so profoundly affected, falling ill shortly after and rapidly losing weight as their health declined. Amidst this turmoil, my six children, ranging from newborn to six years old, required constant attention and care. Despite carrying the heavy burden of losing her beloved sister and closest confidante, Negawr courageously shouldered the responsibility of caring for everyone. With Beeta's unwavering support, she adeptly managed the household tasks and held the family together in a time of agony.

I toiled harder as my work stretched late into the night. Uncle Kia's once boundless energy had waned, and although he was eager, he lacked the strength to engage in the lengthy and frequent social services he had dedicated himself to throughout his life. To alleviate his stress, I took on the tasks that demanded his attention, allowing him to grieve and recuperate.

As the first anniversary of Zivar's passing drew near, we awaited the arrival of my seventh child. While I valued Beeta's commitment and our fulfillment of marital obligations, our connection seemed to lack depth beyond the routines of daily life.

It had been close to a decade since my arrival in Sawmawn, a period that felt like a lifetime. Negawr remained unmarried.

"Oh, Lord, so much has transpired. You Know me better than I understand myself. I have entered marriage twice, experienced the loss of a wife, and now anticipate the arrival of my seventh child, all in accordance with Your Will. After all these events, could I even be a viable option for Negawr? Yet, I cannot help but ponder why she has turned away from suitors who seemed most suitable. My Lord, show me the path You Wish for me to follow. I surrender to Your Divine Will. Please lead me towards that which brings what You will be Pleased with."

In our last meeting by the spring, her words about the passage of time resonated deeply: "Seven years will pass before you know it."

Indeed, those seven years slipped by faster than I could comprehend. She carried a heavy burden, juggling responsibilities from tending to her ailing parents to nurturing my children and maintaining the unity of our family.

"My Lord, You have ordained Negawr as my soulmate. Please grant me a sign to discern whether she awaits me in Your infinite mercy. I have no right to prolong her wait beyond our designated time. Oh Lord,

You are my Witness. Her heavenly love resonates more deeply in my heart than ever despite the worldly distractions that surround me. You know, my Lord, that my affection for her transcends mere worldly desires. But do I possess the worthiness to have her by my side for the remainder of my life?"

I must have a private conversation with Negawr. She deserves to know that she still holds a special place in my heart and that I have not forgotten.

Chapter 29 Fulfilling a Covenant

O n the early morning of the tenth anniversary of my encounter with Negawr at the gate, I ventured towards the spring with a heart heavy with longing. Deep down, I knew she wouldn't be there, for I had implored her not to wait for me seven years ago.

The sky above, a painted masterpiece unfolding before sunrise, stood as the sole dynamic element in a landscape suspended in time since our last meeting. The ethereal symphony of birdsong, a timeless refrain that swirled on the morning breeze, seemed to echo the very essence of that unforgettable day we had shared.

After all those years and changes, my heart raced within my chest at the possibility of reconnecting with Negawr in a secluded moment. The prospect of reigniting our dialogue about "us" stirred a whirlwind of emotions that I had painstakingly buried in the depths of my memory.

"Oh God, this must truly be a glimpse of Your heavenly realm on earth. The tranquility of this place has been a longing in my soul for far too long. This spot, our sanctuary, and even this seat all hold memories that have stood the test of time. I hope that

Negawr would not mind finding me here, waiting. Surely, she will come for water soon. Does she recall this day?"

Lost in my reflections, I lost track of time as I sat in my usual spot.

"Good morning, Sir. Behzawd."

Startled, I rose abruptly from my reverie, anxious about whether she had caught wind of my innermost thoughts.

"Good morning, Miss Negawr. It's a pleasure to see you." I greeted her from the bottom of my heart.

She gently placed the water pitcher down on the ground before stepping over to take her seat, "It has been quite some time since you last graced this place with your presence, Sr.," she murmured once she settled in.

My heart swelled with hope as I stood there, yearning for a sign that she, too, remembered the significance of this day. Our eyes met shyly, conveying unspoken sentiments.

"Yes, I was just reflecting on that myself. I did not wish to intrude," I replied as I returned to my seat, enveloped in a sense of nostalgia.

We turned our panicked gazes into the tranquil water in a moment of silence. Tearful, like two friends who had found each other after a painful and arduous separation.

"My dear Miss Negawr, I ache to assist you in finding a life brimming with fulfillment. Your dedication and hard work merit the joy of starting your own family," my heartfelt words were uttered from a deep sense of empathy and longing.

The weight of unspoken emotions lingered in the air as her unwavering gaze beckoned me to speak further in a serene and contemplative manner.

"May I ask as to why you have declined the proposals of your suitors? There have been numerous honorable gentlemen who could bring you happiness," I ventured with genuine curiosity and concern.

Immediately, regret washed over me as I realized my words could have been misconstrued, potentially causing her pain. Embarrassed by the unintended implication, I found myself unable to meet her gaze, and my eyes cast downward in shame.

Her angelic innocence was overwhelming.

"I did not desire anyone else, Sr. Behzawd," she spoke with certainty. Her angelic innocence exuded a sense of overwhelming purity that tugged tighter at my heartstrings.

"Oh, my dear Negawr, I am filled with deep remorse if my mere presence has inadvertently caused you distress or, worse, tormented you with my mere existence. Life's twists and turns have led me astray, showering me with unexpected surprises and gifts along the way," I confessed, my voice tinged with a mix of regret and self-reflection.

"You are the rock of this family. Your presence has nurtured my growth in ways I never could have fathomed," she expressed with a deep sense of gratitude and sincerity.

An unspoken bond between us conveyed the joy of our shared present moments, enveloped in the tranquil sounds of the water and the birds.

"My dear, Miss Negawr, how could words do justice more than all this? A divine symphony of nature that speaks the truth of our silence," I mused with a sense of wonder and appreciation.

"Indeed, God speaks when we lend an ear," she replied from her spiritual connection.

"Miss Negawr, I do not know where to begin. My seventh child will soon arrive. I have walked down the aisle twice, and today, I have fulfilled the promise I made to my dearest Uncle," I confessed with a mix of introspection and gratitude.

"Yes, indeed, we have much to be thankful for, Sir Behzawd," she acknowledged with a nod.

"I have been bestowed with abundant grace that is undeniable. However, at this moment, I find myself unsure if I even have the right to pose this crucial question," I admitted with uncertainty.

"Is it something I can assist you with?" she inquired.

"Indeed, you are the only one who could provide the help I need," I replied earnestly.

"Please, tell me." urging with anticipation.

Pausing to gather my courage with a deep breath, "Would you consider accepting my hand in marriage?"

She blushed as our eyes locked in a moment of intense connection. The early morning sun cast a surreal display of light, creating a whimsical atmosphere around us. My head swirled in suspended reality, hanging with the weight of those silent moments.

A bashful smile accentuated her captivating charm

as she gazed at the flowing water in silence.

Suddenly, she rose to her feet, signaling her departure. Panic gripped me as a wave of uncertainty flooded my mind.

I swiftly grabbed the pitcher, filling it with water before placing it before her.

"Thank you, Sir. Behzawd."

"You are most welcome, my dear Miss Negawr," aching to hear her direct response to my proposal, I gathered my courage once more, "Will you do me the great honor of becoming my partner for life, Mis Negawr?" I asked with a pounding heart.

Her response was the same: a tender, bashful smile that spoke volumes beyond her words.

"Let us see what father will say, Sr. Behzawd," as I hung in suspense, "we may hope for a more favorable response this time," she added as she balanced the pitcher atop her head.

With a bittersweet smile, I acknowledged the long and arduous journey we had traversed in silence.

"As you wish, Miss Negawr," I bowed slightly.

"Have a splendid day, Sir Behzawd," with a gentle smile, she bid farewell.

"And you as well, my dear one."

Our parting words carried a sense of hope, understanding, and mutual respect, encapsulating the unspoken bond between us.

I walked alongside her for a few paces before coming to a halt, allowing her to continue on her way.

"Peace be with you," I offered.

"Peace and blessings," she replied softly.

My heart ached with anticipation as she faded into the distance, yet a sense of contentment dominated my thoughts as I reflected on the memory of her warm, tender smile.

"Thank you, O Lord, for her unwavering patience and steadfast presence in my life throughout these years. Please grant us Your blessing for a union in marriage to serve You together as Your humble servants. If it pleases You, we shall be forever grateful. Grant her eternal happiness, allow me to stand by her side in unwavering devotion to You, and in piety, if it pleases You, O Lord ..."

I whispered prayers without ceasing, seeking divine guidance and a shower of blessings for our future together.

Chapter 30 Union at Last

As I grappled with doubts about my own qualifications, a stark realization of my inadequacy to be Negawr's chosen partner confronted me. Her presence exuded an aura of awe-inspiring grace, evoking the magnificence of creation. Wherever she went, she sprinkled joy with a divine touch. The question of whether I was worthy of being her other half weighed heavily upon me, a struggle to comprehend.

On the other hand, almost 4 years after Zivar's death, Uncle and Banoo's spirits, burdened by the weight of Zivar's absence, remained ensnared in the clutches of grief.

In the midst of this inner turmoil, my profound aspiration to unite with Negawr shimmered a beacon of hope, capable of illuminating the hearts of all touched by grief, bringing solace through the radiance of Negawr's joy. My deepest longing to uplift and mend spirits lay in the realization of my dream and the transformative power of my love with the potential to transcend the family's shared sorrow, nurturing happiness and unity in its wake.

Moreover, I owed it to everyone that "if Negawr

had chosen to wait for me over her most qualified suitors, I am compelled to ensure that I brought her the same joy and fulfillment that she graciously bestowed upon my life and the lives of others."

Determined to face challenges and be united with my soulmate, I endeavored to embody Negawr's perfection in my approach to rejuvenate energies and uplift spirits.

One late afternoon, clad in a fitting white and blue ensemble, I made my way to discuss my heart's utmost important matter with Uncle Kia. The garden was alive with the backdrop of children's laughter and playful chatter as Uncle Kia sat in his favored spot, engrossed in the pages of a book.

"Peace and Blessings, my dearest Uncle."

As he closed the book, he lifted his head to meet my eyes, "Peace and Blessings to you, my son. It is good to see you."

His subtle smile as he looked me over sparked a wonder within me, pondering whether he, too, drew parallels to our meeting seven years ago.

With reverence, I kissed his hand before taking a seat on the stone-carved bench facing him across from a small pedestal table.

"I am happy to see you, Uncle. I don't get to see you as much as I wish. How are you doing?"

"Thank God, may God Bless you, my son. I am fine, and you look heavenly."

"Thank you, Uncle, you are most kind. All my blessings come from being near you."

"Oh, Behzawd, my dearest companion, your presence has truly been a radiant blessing upon me and this whole town. I don't know what I would have done without you."

"My dearest Uncle, you supported me when I needed help and guided me to maturity. To you, I praise God for you beyond what words can convey. May the heavens above bear witness to my unwavering devotion to your kindness and wisdom."

With the sudden joyous laughter of playing children, we instinctively turned towards the source, where innocent games unfolded in all their delightful splendor.

I regarded the carefree laughter of the children as a promising sign to uplift Uncle from his sorrows.

Taking a deep breath, I initiated, "Dear Uncle, I am deeply grateful for the trust you bestowed upon me with Zivar. May her soul rest in peace. She was not just a devoted wife and an extraordinary woman, but she was also a dear friend to me. Her presence was a precious gift to the world, yet she departed from us far too soon. I humbly seek your forgiveness for not being there more present to ease the void left by her absence for you and Lady Banoo."

"Oh, no, no, please do not burden yourself with such thoughts. You have already done more than I could ever request, my son. Zivar was truly a divine blessing," he expressed softly, wiping away his tears with the sleeves of his garment.

"I am a lucky father to have had her for the time I did. She must be happy in heaven. Even her memories fill me with joy." he continued, his gaze drifting to a distant corner of the garden before returning to me. I listened attentively, offering nods of empathy from time to time.

"Yes, Uncle, she was a true blessing then and continues to be one through her memories and the children she left behind. I am grateful for your guidance; without it, I would not have realized."

"She was indeed a great blessing, my son, and you were a perfect complement to her. It is a pity she had to depart so soon," he reflected somberly.

We mourned in silence for a while, observing the

children playing in the distance as the birds sang their final melodies of the day.

"Uncle, would you mind if we discussed some plans for the future?"

"Of course, please proceed. What is on your mind?"

"It has been a decade since I came here,"

"Yes, my son, it seems like just yesterday,"

"I am truly grateful, Uncle, for every moment of it. You have provided for me, cared for me, and bestowed upon me the honor of being your son-in-law. May God reward you abundantly in the hereafter,"

"You have been a true blessing to have by my side, my son,"

"Thank you, Uncle. Now, I must seek your blessing on an important matter,"

"Anything at all, my son, just ask,"

Summoning my courage, I paused briefly, then took a deep breath.

"May I have the honor of asking for Miss Negawr's hand in marriage, Sir?"

"Oh, yes, my son. I have not overlooked our agreement. Blessings be upon you and Negawr. I will speak to her about your wish,"

It was getting dark. I accompanied Uncle to his home, bidding him farewell with a kiss on his hand at the foot of the stairs before making my way back home.

The following day, after completing my tasks, I strolled alongside one of the shepherds as he guided his herd back from the fields. After he secured the barn gates, we parted ways, each continuing on our respective paths as the sun dipped toward the horizon.

I spotted Uncle Kia standing on his veranda in the distance. With a wave, I made my way over to greet him. I saluted him again before closing the gap between us.

"Hello, Uncle, how are you?"

Returning my smile, Uncle Kia, always eager to share good news, could hardly contain his excitement as he replied.

"Praise God, I am very well, thank you. Congratulations, my son, your proposal has been accepted,"

Overwhelmed with happiness, I hurriedly skipped

the steps to reach him faster, wrapping my arms around him in a tight embrace.

"Thank you, Uncle. Thank you," I expressed gratefully as he patted my back, and we embraced in a warm hug filled with shared joy and blessings.

"Thank you, Uncle. Thank you," I repeated with gratitude, sealing our joy with a warm hug.

"God bless you, my son,"

At long last, there was no barrier standing between Negawr and me. Overwhelmed with emotion, I kissed Uncle's face and then his hands, expressing my deep appreciation and respect.

"I will cherish and protect her with my life, Uncle. I promise you that. Thank you, Sir,"

"I know you do, my son. God bless you."

Preparations swiftly unfolded, and within days, Negawr and I were united in marriage amidst a public ceremony. The celebration marked the first time the entire village came together since Zivar's passing.

As the wedding festivities came to a close, our guests escorted us to the front of the newly completed northern building that would serve as our new home.

As we ascended the stairs, Uncle Kia and Lady

Banoo close behind, I stepped into the happiest chapter of my life.

As we settled into our new routine, Negawr radiated joy and contentment. She remained steadfast in her priorities, dedicated to caring for others, especially Beeta's emotional well-being. Time and again, she reminded and encouraged me to prioritize quality time with Beeta as my partner.

Negawr and I found ourselves busier than ever, engrossed in our respective responsibilities – from attending family and social gatherings to overseeing the village's agricultural endeavors and proper distribution of goods. Despite our hectic schedules, we treasured every fleeting moment we shared together, savoring the rare opportunities that allowed us to be in each other's presence.

Years drifted by. Beeta blessed me with a second son. Negawr and Beeta gracefully navigated the intricate web of family matters, tending to the needs of my eight children with unwavering care and devotion. Standing by Negawr's side brought a profound sense of fulfillment to my life despite the inevitable challenges that accompanied raising a large family.

Driven not only by societal norms and expectations but also by her own deep yearning, Negawr longed to bear a child of our own. Slowly, she found herself entangled in a cruel web of malicious whispers and taunts from the townspeople, who labeled her as barren and incapable of giving birth.

"She is barren."

"She is not capable of giving birth."

"She cannot give her husband a child."

"She cannot fulfill her husband's needs."

Despite the harsh and hurtful words that encircled her, Negawr's resilience and inner strength radiated through as she faced them with unwavering grace and dignity.

The very same women who once revered Negawr for her remarkable qualities now made her feel inadequate with their malicious gossip.

These long-time residents of Sawmawn, who had thrived for generations in prosperity and tranquility, found solace in the art of gossip. Their narrow perspectives shaped their opinions on what life should or should not entail. In their judgmental eyes, our deep, loving relationship carried little significance. Negawr felt compelled to bow to the relentless scrutiny and criticism of the townspeople in order to demonstrate her worth and love to the entire town.

Chapter 31 Improper Gift

As the summer months drew to a close, the town hummed with anticipation akin to the eve of a grand festival. A decade had passed since our union, yet the pitter-patter of tiny feet had not graced our home. With a brood of my own from a previous marriage, society's whispers painted Negawr as the bearer of barrenness, thus thrusting upon her the onus of proving her devotion to me before its watchful eyes.

As the clock neared midnight, the moon's gentle glow painted elongated shadows across the room. Negawr moved gracefully about, completing her final tasks before embracing the beckoning call of bed. Nestled upon the bed, I absorbed her lively accounts of the imminent holiday revelries.

"Tomorrow holds the promise of becoming a day enshrined in the collective memory of our town, and I ardently pray for you as well, my beloved," she whispered tenderly, planting a kiss on my brow as she settled beside me.

"Every moment spent by your side is a cherished memory, my dearest," I murmured, relishing the comforting warmth of her presence in the tranquil embrace of the night.

"Mine as well, my love, yet I yearn to fashion this one into an exceptionally extraordinary affair. A decade has slipped through our grasp so fast."

I drew her close into the circle of my arm, a silent embrace affirming her words. "Every facet of this world holds significance when you grace my side. I long for naught but your presence, my love. Simply remain near me like this, forever intertwined, won't you?"

She smiled, nestling deeper into the cradle of my arms. A hint of longing lingered in her voice.

"For you, I shall forever be just a heartbeat away, but I yearn to proclaim it to the world," she murmured softly.

"Why must you feel compelled to display our love to the world? Is our life together not enough to kindle your happiness?" I inquired with sincere concern.

"Well, it would be easier to convey it even to myself if you accepted a gift I have for you," she proposed.

"My dearest, I require nothing but your presence. You are my everything,"

"This gift is for me, a symbol of my affection for you,"

"Ah, so you are gifting me for yourself?" I replied.

Our joyous laughter filled the room.

"Yes, how about that?" she teased.

Realizing her earnestness, I chose to prioritize her happiness over any debate.

"If you vow to remain by my side, then I accept whatever you offer. Are you happy?"

"Really? You mean it?" she inquired, her eyes searching mine for reassurance.

"Of course, have I ever given you a reason to doubt my sincerity?"

"No, my dear, merely seeking to satisfy my heart," she confessed.

"Without a doubt. With you by my side, I possess all I need to brave the world. I love you, and I treasure any gift from you as a part of you. Do you trust my words?"

She embraced me tight with warmth and gratitude.

"Of course, my love, please forgive me. I simply

longed for your reassurance," she whispered.

"Sweetheart, I solemnly vow to accept your gift with utmost joy."

"Thank you, my love, you are my dreams come true, every moment,"

With a new excitement, she rolled onto her stomach to face me. Propped up on her elbows, her head loomed above mine, our eyes locking in the soft moonlight. A subtle glimmer danced in her eyes with unspoken words. In a hesitating pause, she traced her fingers across my hand with uncertainty. She was mustering to voice her thoughts with deep breaths.

"You know ... *pause*... *deep breath*... we've been caught up in the whirlwind of busyness and distractions. *pause* I fear I may have fallen short of meeting all your needs."

Before she could continue, I interjected, "Sweetheart, you fulfill my every need beyond my wildest dreams. You have never fallen short of anything, my love. Why do you even think such?"

"Please, listen. This is truly important to me."

"Okay, go on," I urged, eager to hear her thoughts.

"You know Mina, my maid,"

"Yes, she seems to be one of your trusted assistants."

"Yes, she sure is, not just a trusted assistant but also wise, young, and beautiful. I believe she has the potential to bear healthy and strong children. I would like you to accept her hand in marriage as my gift to you, my love," she proposed earnestly.

Shocked and repulsed by the suggestion, "This is no jest, my dear. I am wholeheartedly content with our life together, and I have no desire for more children unless they are with you."

"Sweetheart, your happiness matters most to me. With a man as remarkable as you, the world deserves to have hundreds of children to carry on your legacy," she persisted.

Feeling hurt and insulted with a reflective expression of dismay, "Is this how little you value me? Have you grown weary of our bond? Am I a burden when all I desire is to remain close to you, to cherish you? Amidst all the people in the world, you, of all, should understand the depth of my love for you. How could you even entertain the thought of me marrying another woman after everything we've shared and overcome together?"

"Hush, my love, this is not to upset you. Remember

your promise," she whispered with a pleading tone in her voice.

Suppressing the torrent of questions swirling in my mind, I reflected on the rumors and gossip she must have been exposed to. It pained me to think of the harsh realities of the world she had been living in.

I held her close, breathing in her scent as I pressed a tender kiss behind her ears and on her neck, my heart heavy with both sorrow and affection for the sacrifice she believed she needed to make.

"Is this once again about the words and opinions of others? Why do you let them trouble you, my love? Are you not content with me?"

"You know how content I am with you, my love, and how my happiness knows no bounds. But I am aware of my inability to give you children despite my fervent desire. Please accept my gift of love." she pleaded with vulnerability.

Our tender embrace and fervent kisses, ignited by the depths of our love, affirmed our unwavering dedication to each other and our readiness to make sacrifices without hesitation.

Reclining beside her, enveloped in a serene peace that I held most dear, was a sense of tranquility that I was determined to safeguard at all costs. Reflecting silently on the weight of each of my two options, I understood that turning down her proposal would undoubtedly cause her heartache while embracing the idea of marrying another woman might bring about her anguish despite her current enthusiasm.

Her gentle whisper interrupted my thoughts. "My love, we have faced the most formidable challenges together; this is merely another hurdle to conquer. You see, in our customs, a woman's gift of another woman to her husband is seen as proof of her profound love for him."

"Wow! That is so cruel and unjust," I exclaimed.

"Perhaps it appears that way to you, my love, but its wisdom truly astonishes me. Consider this - as humans, we unlock our ultimate potential when we wholeheartedly embrace selflessness. If you were to accept my gift, you would be assisting me in ascending to heights that would otherwise be beyond the reach of my soul."

As her head rested on my chest, she continued to confide in me while I was lost in contemplation. A tumultuous debate raged within my mind. "Should I let the cruel whispers of others continue to shatter her heart? Or should I uphold my misguided promise and play a part in breaking it myself?"

"Will you keep your promise? Please?" she whispered as a myriad of thoughts raced through my mind. "Altering the mindset of the villagers required intergenerational changes and a continuous battle against a superstitious mentality that exploited beliefs in demonic forces. I was certain that such societal norms could serve as a groundwork for leading humanity astray and perpetuating injustices against the vulnerable."

Just when I thought she had drifted off to sleep, I felt her tear drop on my skin. Embracing her tightly with a gentle kiss on her head, I could not bear her tears.

"My love, you are crying! Come, I will do it to silence the wagging tongues, but their gossip is baseless nonsense. You should not have to endure its sting. I accept your gift. Would you not shed any more tears, please!"

"Okay, I'll try, thank you for accepting my gift, my love,"

She embraced me tightly as I wrapped my arms around her.

"Under one condition," I demanded.

"Sure, anything," she lifted her head to look me in

the eyes.

"Remember, you are my one true soulmate. My Negawr, you must remain by my side, always, will you?"

"I will always be close to you, my Behzawd," she vowed.

As we sealed our deal and drifted off to sleep, I realized the immense social pressure and the enormity of her sacrifice in upholding peace within the confines of societal conventions.

The next day, during the grand seasonal celebration, Negawr took my hand, standing next to her, and beckoned Mina to join us.

"My dear friends and family, I am thrilled to share some wonderful news with all of you today. I invite you to join me in congratulating the union of our esteemed Sir Behzawd and our cherished friend, Miss Mina."

The crowd hailed with cheers and good wishes as Negawr placed Mina's hand in mine. With Negawr having proved her love for me, a sense of contentment washed over everyone, as if a weight had been lifted off their minds, allowing them to resume celebrating the event with renewed vigor.

At the conclusion of the grand festivities, a select few of our nearest relatives accompanied Mian and me to our newly appointed abode - the converted guesthouse meticulously prepared by Negawr as part of her generous gift package.

As the days turned into weeks, months, and years, Negawr nudged me to devote more time to Mina, emphasizing the importance of her happiness in recognition of our shared journey.

I was resolute in my desire for Mina to never feel neglected or adrift in a sea of emotions. Loving her required no exertion, for her authenticity, benevolence, modesty, and commitment enveloped my heart in a warm embrace of appreciation and gratitude.

As the second year came to an end, we welcomed Mina's firstborn son. Two years later, another son graced our lives, and after an additional two years, a precious daughter completed the trio of Mina's children, marking the fulfillment of a joyous beginning for the entire family.

Negawr, my closest confidant, took the lead, bearing the responsibility of nurturing our family bonds in unity. My heart brimmed with joy and gratitude for the eleven children who served as a beacon of hope, promising a future abundant with love and cherished moments for every member of our expansive family.

Chapter 32 New Dynamics

Uncle Kia and Banoo never quite recovered from the heart-wrenching loss of Zivar. Nevertheless, Uncle Kia persisted in shouldering his share of responsibilities, embodying a tenacious work ethic that mirrored that of my dear father, whom I missed dearly.

Recognizing the enduring emotional battle he grappled with; I made it my mission to alleviate Uncle's burden by taking on his tasks to grant him a respite from superfluous concerns.

"Dearest Uncle, it is time for you to retire. Let me and the others shoulder these chores. Your legacy is secure; you have given enough," I begged him with sincerity.

Driven by a deep-rooted work ethic, he remained steadfast in carrying out chores to the extent of his capabilities. His unwavering devotion stood as a poignant homage to my beloved father, whose absence continued to weigh heavily on my heart. In moments of reflection, I keenly yearned to share my blessings with my parents and siblings.

We reshaped the dynamics of our household to nurture a climate of peace and acceptance for the grieving hearts of Lady Banoo and Uncle Kia. I assumed the responsibility of supervising village-wide affairs, including the management of farms, manufacturing, distribution, and social commitments.

Meanwhile, Negawr devoted herself tirelessly to the meticulous upkeep of both familial and communal affairs, ensuring the welfare of every individual within our family and the village. Her unwavering concern for the needs of others left her content only when everyone was happy.

Negawr created a robust support system to care for her parents and the younger children while managing her village-wide duties. To counteract the proliferation of sorcery that had gained traction in recent years, she orchestrated events in collaboration with my other wives, Beeta and Min. Together, they orchestrated initiatives aimed at raising awareness and uplifting the spirits of the community in a collective effort to combat the sorcerers' insidious drain on the energy and morality of the unsuspecting members of the village.

Unknowingly, we were gradually drifting apart physically as we each navigated the responsibilities that entwined our lives with the happiness of those around us.

Chapter 33 The Growing Town

In response to the burgeoning population, a collective endeavor was undertaken to cultivate the indigenous knowledge and talents of the townspeople. Collaborating closely with a coalition of scholars and the venerable sages of the community, we formulated a set of guiding principles aimed at effectively stewarding the town's resources to elevate both its economic vitality and social harmony.

Our collective aspiration was to foster self-reliance and usher in an era of abundance by optimizing the town's production, distribution, and manufacturing processes while advancing education and fostering a sense of communal solidarity rooted in faith.

Over the course of a decade-long journey filled with trials and triumphs, we unearthed the enchanting power of incentives, offering individual farmers the opportunity to claim ownership stakes and reap the rewards under the vigilant guidance of the collective.

The outcomes were nothing short of remarkable - a delightful surge in economic prosperity. Sawmawn swiftly ascended to the status of a prominent exporter and distributor of agricultural commodities within the region.

During the tranquil hours of the night, while the world slumbered, Negawr remained my steadfast companion in prayer as together we sought closeness to the Divine. She offered heartfelt supplications to fill the silence left by my unspoken thoughts.

O Lord, instill peace in this world, You who are the Sole Refuge, bless us with a righteous successor to guide Your faithful, and in Your mercy, lead us to stay steadfast on the path to Your Divine presence, seeking only to fulfill Your Will.

Chapter 34 Departure of Divine Presence

After twenty-five years of quietly mourning the loss of Zivar, Banoo and Uncle Kia had a sudden decline in their health that sent shockwaves of fear through the village. Crowds of his devoted followers flocked to his bedside daily, their hearts heavy with the looming specter of loss.

One fateful day, as I sat vigil by Uncle Kia's bedside, he mustered the strength to ask for all visitors to leave. With his hand clasped in mine, he drew me closer, placing his other hand on top of ours against his chest. Despite the struggle to keep his eyes open, a glimmer of profound contentment danced in his gaze as he spoke with great effort and sincerity.

"My son, the time has come for me to leave this earthly abode. I entrust you and Negawr with the responsibility of guiding people along The Straight Path. I have earnestly implored them to embrace faith through the years. While a few have answered this call, many cling to fragile faith and continue to reside in ignorance. I leave praying for the Grace of God to awaken them before it is too late. I fear their potential loss..."

I listened attentively. He was concerned for the salvation of his people.

"My dearest son, I am prepared to dance into the arms of my Beloved," he spoke with fervor, "Oh, Lord, safeguard your people from temptations, enlighten their hearts to comprehend that this life is merely a transient stop on the unswerving journey to Your everlasting Joy. Unveil to them the ultimate Truth," he paused in between words to catch his breaths, and his eyes drifted closed from exhaustion.

"My Behzawd," he called out with a sense of urgency.

"Yes, Uncle, I am here, listening," in a swift response.

"Prepare them for the reckoning of the hereafter before the veils are lifted, and they must answer for their deeds and for what they have done with the blessings bestowed upon them in this world. If only they would surrender to The Merciful God, Who is closer to them than their own jugular vein, more compassionate than their most loving mother..."

He spoke urgently. I gently caressed his resting hand on his chest for soothing assurance, to no avail.

As he lingered in a prolonged pause, I was

captivated by the radiant glow in the air above him, most intense around his head. I wiped my teary eyes with my sleeve to sharpen my vision.

The radiance appeared as a golden magnetic field pulsating with flowing green and orange waves. I felt the rhythm of his pulse, watching his veins as if they were streams of divine love connected to my soul.

"… my dear son … thank you, forgive me, praise be to God, The Lord, and Cherisher of the worlds, may God keep you on His Chosen Path, … thank you," his whispers drifted.

I pressed my eyes shut to dispel the tears blurring my vision, wiping them away as I strained to hear his breathing.

His voice fell silent. His grip loosened on my hand. With closed eyes, his face was frozen in a smile that captured one of his most endearing expressions.

"Uncle … my dearest Uncle," I whispered with great sorrow.

He was gone. His serene smile was a comforting sign of his flight to "dance to meet his Beloved."

I wept as I laid my head on his chest, mourning in a hushed whisper, "Oh Lord, bless his soul. He was a loving father and my greatest mentor. Thank You,

Lord, for gracing me with the gift of his presence. Please lead me to follow in his footsteps and grant me the fortitude to endure for the sake of his loved ones... Oh, my dear uncle."

Negawr entered the room. Overwhelmed with sorrow, tears flew down her face as she leaned over Uncle, embracing and kissing his face. I reached out and took her in my arms as she rested her head against my chest.

More individuals began to enter the room, distraught, their tears mingling in a collective expression of mourning. The entire town was plunged into grief...

Broken hearted Banoo grieved in despair, unable to bear the weight of separation. In her anguish, she longed to have departed before her husband. Unfortunately for everyone surviving, her fervent wish was granted quickly as she passed away within a month while in Negawr's embrace.

The divine presence of Uncle and Banoo was abruptly snatched away one after another, leaving a profound void in our lives. The village draped itself in mourning black, a poignant tribute to their memory, and continued to mourn the absence of their elegant presence for years to come.

In due time, Negawr came to accept the bitter reality of her parents' absence. Together, we grieved, finding comfort in one another's presence as we carried out our daily tasks. Our shared journey of mourning and the alchemy of healing forged bonds of strength and resilience between us that surpassed our wildest dreams. With each passing day, our connection deepened, blossoming into a mature companionship that we never knew was possible before.

Chapter 35 A Miracle

As my youngest children, now in their twenties, had settled in the town with their own families, Negawr and I found ourselves blessed with more opportunities to spend our precious free time together.

After forty-five years of marriage, we were enveloped in a love that burned more passionately than ever before. I couldn't help but notice the ethereal glow in her eyes and the articulated aura of grace that surrounded her. She appeared even more radiant and beautiful than the day we first met at the gate over fifty-five years ago. I was overjoyed with the thought that she had embraced the fact of not having children and had found contentment in the life we had built together.

One late evening, Negawr and I were walking back home from a town meeting. The full moon illuminated the world as if it were daylight, casting a magical glow over everything it touched. My arm was wrapped around her shoulders, and her hand rested gently on my back as we marveled at the splendors of the night.

Suddenly, she stopped and turned to face me.

"Behzawd," in her soft voice.

"Yes, dear," I replied curiously.

"Do you believe in miracles?" she asked, her loving eyes tugging at my heartstrings.

"Of course, my love. Everything we see is a miracle, isn't it?"

"No, I mean an extraordinary miracle," she clarified.

"God Creates as He Pleases. When He Says Be, it Is. Miracles are His specialty, my love. Even the extraordinary ones, right?" I acknowledged the divine power that orchestrates all affairs.

"Yes, they are, as special as a child in our age?" she mused, drawing parallels between the miraculous and accepted truth.

"Sure. If He Pleases, that is possible too. Nothing is difficult for God,"

"Yes, nothing, not even our baby in my womb," she affirmed with a mix of hope and longing.

Worried, I looked her in the eyes, which shone with a radiant, angelic glow in the moonlight. My heart ached at the thought that the pain of not having a child still lingered within her. At that moment, I held her close, kissing her tenderly and wrapping her in a comforting embrace, hoping to ease her pain.

"Sure, even a baby in your womb is possible, my love. That is easy for God," I whispered with a kiss.

"Yes, so easy for God, I feel our baby inside me,"

"Oh, my dearest, what are you saying?" I asked with mixed emotions of worry, disbelief, and overwhelming happiness.

"Yes, our precious baby! Nestled within my womb, alive and thriving! I feel our baby inside me, my love," she whispered in awe.

"Praise be to God. Oh, Lord, Divine Creator, please make our child the one who is submitted to Your Will," I murmured, embracing her as praise and gratitude poured out from the depths of my heart.

I was compelled to bow down in humble prostration... The Merciful and Gracious God had indeed blessed her deepest desire. I had been steadfast in praying fervently for her wishes to come true before, but I never dared to petition for such a singular favor if it lay beyond His divine plan, for we had willingly surrendered to God's Will and the abundance of blessings He had bestowed upon us already.

As Negawr ascended from her reverent pose, we settled upon the chilled stone pavers with hands entwined in a shared rapture, delighted by the mysterious beauty of the night unfolding around us.

Suddenly, her delicate condition dawned on me, prompting me to gently lift her into my arms.

"Sweetheart, you should not be sitting on this cold surface. Let's head home. You must be exhausted,"

"I am fine, my love. I can walk, really," she whispered with a smile, her voice filled with gratitude for my concern.

Giggling, with her still in my arms, we shared a long embrace. Eventually, I gently lowered her to the ground, and hand in hand, we made our way home. The moon bore witness to our praises for God and joyful whispers.

"Oh, Lord, all praise belongs to You. Please guide our child to be among Your righteous believers, devoted to serving You in Truth. May this new generation be one of piety, devoted to worshipping You and seeking to please You above all else ..."

Negawr deserved to be happy y, and witnessing her joy brought me immense delight.

Aside from the old age, for reasons unknown, her pregnancy grew increasingly complex as time passed. By the final stretch of the third trimester, her condition took a perilous turn, necessitating round-the-clock observation and bed rest.

The fear of losing her was a haunting specter, but before long, she safely delivered a healthy, beautiful baby boy.

"Oh, Behzawd, he is the fruit of our love. I pray to God that he grows to be as wise as you, destined to lead with virtue and fulfill the divine purpose of his creation. What shall we name him? Can you think of a name that befits the noblest of characters?"

"He looks like a perfect angel! His presence is a pure blessing, and his birth is a miracle! What do you think of PawkZawd or Parsaw for his name?" I suggested.

"I love both.! They are both perfect names, born pure, and live with piety! It's a tough choice! Let's name him PawkZawd for our close circle, you and I, and Parsaw for others," she declared with joy.

"Indeed, PawkZawd, born from our pure love, and Parsaw, may he embrace piety throughout his life! So be it, God Willing," I affirmed, supporting her choices wholeheartedly.

PawkZawd's arrival ushered in a celestial aura of joy that not only enveloped his immediate environment but extended beyond any boundaries known to the village world. As he blossomed, he bore a striking resemblance to Negawr in both features and traits, embodying a divine beauty that rendered him utterly lovable and endearing.

Even before he turned two, PawkZawd developed a fondness for playing by the stream. His insatiable curiosity about nature, birds, and aquatic life kept Negawr and me thoroughly engaged.

His presence in our spring site's serene setting transformed it into an even more cherished and unforgettable place for both of us.

Chapter 36 Longing of Our Hearts

In the soft whispers of Uncle Kia and Lady Banoo's lingering essence in Sawmawn, Negawr and I stood poised on the precipice of a new chapter, where the intertwined threads of love and memory transcended the confines of birthplaces and past generations.

With a voice that resonated with both determination and tenderness, Negawr proposed a journey to Mihan, my birthplace, where my dear parents and siblings dwelled. In her words, the weight of the past and the shimmering promise of the future converged to shape the path forward for our children.

"Behzawd, my dearest, with no grandparents to enrich our children's lives, this is a pivotal crossroads that holds the key to their happy future. Let us venture on a pilgrimage to Mihan and bask in the divine blessings of your parents' presence," Negawr expressed with reverence and longing.

"Yes, my love, the void left by the absence of Uncle Kia, Lady Banoo, and Zivar will reverberate through many generations. May the divine grace forever shine upon their souls. Their absence has rendered this place into a hollow echo of memories. It is indeed a splendid idea to hasten on to revel in the cherished company of my parents if you believe we can depart without regret for leaving this place behind," I lamented as the yearning for my parents' presence tugged at my heartstrings, even as time seemed to slip away.

Contemplating the profound impact of parents, I added, "Parents are the ethereal architects of our lives. Despite the vast distance that separated them, it was my parents' unseen guidance that brought me to this sacred land nearly six decades ago, where destiny led me to find you, my beloved."

Negawr resonated with my thoughts, expressing, "I often find myself pondering how different my journey would have been without you here, my beloved Behzawd."

Thus began the journey towards my parents' abode, a sacred pilgrimage steeped in memories and revelations, introducing our children to their paternal heritage that awaited them. The echoes of the past carried whispers of both loss and yearning, while the horizon of the future gleamed with the light of rejuvenation, spanning the divide between grief and the embrace of fresh blessings and rekindled ties.

"I do have one concern, my love," I voiced with skepticism, "that you may find it challenging to part ways with all that you hold dear – your home and the people you cherish."

"Not at all, my dear. Home resides where our hearts are. I find contentment wherever I am as long as I am by your side and with PawkZawd. Perhaps we should gather the thoughts of our other children as well, offering them the choice to relocate to your hometown permanently," Negawr proposed with thoughtful consideration.

"Oh, you never cease to amaze me, my Negawr," I exclaimed with a twinkle of an eye.

"We should plan to go, whether for a visit or for a more permanent move," she suggested with excitement.

"Just envision the sheer delight of our children being with my parents. Oh, my parents will be thrilled." the happiness that awaits us fills my heart with joy," I mused, unable to control the smile dancing on my lips as I thought of reuniting with my parents and my siblings.

Upon proposing the notion of relocating to Mihan with my ten sons, their initial response was far from enthusiastic.

"Father, this is our home, where we took our first

breaths. It holds all that we know and cherish... You can find comfort here, witnessing your children and grandchildren thrive," they expressed, their words laced with a sense of attachment and nostalgia.

Despite their attempts to dissuade me, urging me to stay rooted in our familiar surroundings, a shift occurred. After days of deliberation and heartfelt conversations amongst themselves, a wave of excitement washed over them at the prospect of embarking on this journey to a new land, viewing it as a thrilling adventure waiting to unfold.

In a matter of weeks, a bustling caravan comprising over seventy members of my family stood poised and prepared to embark on the monumental journey ahead.

Amidst the flurry of final preparations, a familiar face emerged - Hadi, a seasoned local trader known for his frequent travels abroad and intimate knowledge of the region, arrived with a plea to dissuade me from departing upon hearing the news of our impending migration.

"Sir. Behzawd, these people rely on you. We need you here. Please reconsider, maybe just for a short visit and then come back. Allow me to accompany you to Mihan and ensure your safe return when you are ready," Hadi implored sincerely.

"Thank you, Hadi, for your kindness. This decision is not just for my family but also for the greater good of this entire community. It is an opportunity for everyone to reinforce their own resilience and faith as I long to reunite with the other half of my family after so long. My children deserve to bask in the love and wisdom of their grandparents before it is too late," I affirmed with a sense of conviction and resolve.

Eventually, Hadi accepted that my decision was final, "It appears your mind is set, Sir. Allow me the honor of guiding your caravan home to Mihan," he conceded graciously.

"That is truly generous of you, Hadi. Your expertise is a gift we deeply appreciate. My son, Puyaw, will undoubtedly be a valuable asset on this journey as well. Could you coordinate the logistics for our family to venture through the towns via the swiftest and most picturesque routes?" I inquired, sending someone to ask Puyaw to join us.

As Hadi began elucidating, "I have a clear plan in mind regarding the routes we should traverse. Rest assured, it will be a journey that both the young and old members of your family will relish," Puyaw arrived, ready to partake in the discussion.

"Would that be suitable for the young children?" Puyaw asked.

"Oh, certainly! Several of the cities along this picturesque route are located by the sea. The children will absolutely adore it. You," he said, glancing at Puyaw, "will lead the caravan at the front. We require a few additional robust men to protect the flanks and rear of the caravan."

Puyaw could not contain his excitement, exclaiming proudly, "My brothers can handle that. The ten of us should be able to cover the sides, front, and back."

"Fantastic! I'll stay close ahead of you," Hadi replied.

This was my once-in-a-lifetime opportunity to craft indelible memories for my children, grandchildren, and great-grandchildren. They will glean invaluable lessons from their shared adventures, and the memories they forge will guide them wisely through life.

The journey unfolded as an extraordinary expedition deserving its own travel book atlas. While we camped along the way to rest and play, there was a treasure trove of wisdom to amass, knowledge to gather, a tapestry of cultures to immerse in, and awe-inspiring scenery to serve as the backdrop for their unforgettable memories in this remarkable world.

Chapter 37 Arriving Home

As a new dawn broke over the horizon, painting the sky in hues of pink and gold, our journey continued its grand expedition. Pawkzawd nestled between Negawr and me in our cozy two-wheeled carriage cart adorned with a protective canopy. Each day brought new adventures, and when awake, Pawkzawd's excitement radiated as he eagerly assisted me in holding the reins and steering our noble steed.

Star, my loyal thirty-year-old white Arabian horse, commanded our carriage in all her majestic figure with grace and precision. Adorned with a collar that encircled her dished face and a harness that connected her to the cart, she exuded a regal, captivating presence. Her elegant neck arched proudly while her mane shimmered in the sunlight, each silvery gray strand dancing in the wind in celebration. Her cascading gray tail held aloft in a silent proclamation of joy and triumph. The rhythmic prancing of her strong legs and the synchronized movement of the shafts on her sides satisfied a silent, faithful exchange of trust that transcended the paths we had traveled together.

The caravan stretched out like a vibrant mosaic of

colors against the backdrop of the winding road that beckoned us forward into the unknown. With each turn, our hearts swelled with anticipation of novel encounters, the deepening bond that tethered us on this voyage of revelation, and the jubilant prospect of reuniting with beloved souls at the culmination of our expedition.

As the caravan made its way through cities and towns, enduring over five weeks of arduous travel, we finally reached my cherished hometown of Mihan. The afternoon sun hung low in the sky, casting our elongated shadows upon the ancient cobblestone streets that echoed with whispers of history. Filled with a profound sense of awe and reverence for the journey we had undertaken, the dancing embraces of long shadows brought to my mind a mysterious realization of the converging past and present.

As my gaze swept over the familiar buildings, I could not help but notice how the relentless march of time had left its mark, transforming their once-familiar facades into something new and unfamiliar yet undeniably captivating.

The grand landmarks that had once served as distinct beacons, guiding the travelers through the labyrinthine streets of Mihan, now stood shrouded in mystery.

Curious onlookers congregated as our lengthy caravan wound its way through the bustling town, a mesmerizing display of horses, camels, and more than forty carriages that seized the gaze of the beholders. The townsfolk halted their daily pursuits to witness the procession of the travelers as if they were exotic visitors from abroad.

Within the throng, benevolent spirits hurried forth to greet us, their hospitality overflowing and their greetings imbued with warmth. In their gestures, I sensed a profound connection with the hearts of the people who graciously offered us shelter to soothe our weary souls.

The eager welcomers were not only extending hospitality but also seeking to unravel the mystery of our origins.

"Welcome! Do you require lodging?" They inquired as questions grew lauder.

"Where do you come from?"

With each inquiry that was met with a negative response, their curiosity only deepened.

"What is your name?"

"Puyaw, son of Behzawd,"

"Who is your leader?"

"Sr. Behzawd."

"Who? Sr. Behzawd?"

"Oh, my, Sr. Behzawd!"

"Will you stay in Mihan?"

"Yes."

"Would you like to stay at my house?"

"No, thank you. We do not need a place to stay right now."

"My home is yours."

"Thank you. We are here to see Sir Farshawd,"

"Sir Farshawd? Does he know you?"

"Yes, he is my grandfather."

"Oh! Welcome!"

"Good news, good news, the children of Sir Farshawd are here."

As they pieced together the information, the chatter grew louder, filling the air with a sense of realization and excitement.

"Oh, where is Sir. Behzawd?"

"He is here, among us. Do you see that carriage with red and yellow cover?"

The crowd surged towards my carriage; their voices raised in jubilant cries as they spread the word.

"Sir. Farshad's son has come back! Sir Behzawd has come back! Praise God,"

They chanted praises and led the caravan to its destination.

My heart raced as I caught sight of my father's residence complex in the distance.

A group of individuals emerged from a nearby gate, with a woman breaking away from the pack and rushing towards us.

"Could that be …?"

I pulled on the reins, passing them to Negawr, then alighted from the carriage and hurried towards her.

"Oh, Farah! My cherished little sister! Peace be upon you!"

"My Behzawd! You came back! Oh, Lord, praise be unto You."

We embraced as people hailed.

"Oh, my dearest brother."

"Take me to father and mother. How are they?"

"Come, come."

Chapter 38 Six Decades Apart

As the sun dipped low on the horizon, casting long, dramatic shadows across the ancient city, Farah and I strolled ahead, leaving the bustling caravan behind. Caught by emotions, a raw undercurrent choked us beneath the overwhelming happiness that filled the air. Farah, slender yet strong, stood at my shoulder, my arm draped over hers.

Passing through the weathered stone gate, she had emerged from moments before, we stepped into the tranquil embrace of the inner gardens. Memories flooded my mind. I turned back, scanning the crowd for a glimpse of Negawr. The fervent chanting and lively energy of the encircling throng obscured my view.

As I looked up at the window opening, a portal to my last memory from six decades past, there she stood. Time seemed to stand still as she exuded a tranquil grace that had remained etched in my mind all these years. A vision frozen in the sands of time; my mother watched over me with a love that transcended the years.

With a tender kiss on Farah's head, I released her from my grasp, and with a surge of emotion, I ascended the stairs, two at a time, just as I had done in my youth.

Reaching the top, breathless and filled with a sense of urgency, I stood before the open doorway in the presence of my mother. "Peace and Blessings, mother, oh, my dearest mother," we whispered with tears and overflowing emotions.

We embraced as I drank her familiar scent. I pressed kisses to her head, her cheeks, and her hands in dreamlike moments that surpassed any words to speak of.

Tears mingled freely between us, a silent exchange of love and longing that bridged the gap of years apart. With each pause in our embrace, we found ourselves drawn back together, kissing and holding each other as if trying to make up for lost time in a single moment.

Her gentle touch, weathered with age, traced the contours of my face in disbelief as if reassuring herself that it was truly me. "Oh, mother. It is so good to see you," I whispered repeatedly.

She was frail yet most beautiful.

"Yes, my darling, it is a miracle that I can see you again," she said as she looked up to the heavens, "Oh Lord, praise be unto You!"

"Praise be to the Lord," I echoed.

"Oh, my Lord, You have bestowed upon me the precious gift of seeing my Behzawd once more. Thank You, Lord! You have made my deepest dream a reality…" In a chorus of gratitude and praise, a sense of peace settled over us like a gentle caress, calming the storm of emotions that had welled up within.

Brushing away my tears, "Where is father, mother?" I inquired amidst her lingering echoes of gratitude reverberating through the air.

"I am certain he is in peace, my son. May God bless his soul," she replied with a sense of comfort and acceptance.

I sank to the floor beside her, resting my head upon her knees in seeking solace as I grappled with the weight of regret and sorrow, "Oh, my dearest father, please forgive me, for I have come too late," yearning for forgiveness.

As I lifted my gaze, her tear-filled eyes tugged at my heartstrings. Rising to my knees to align myself with her eyes, I enveloped her fragile form within the shelter of my embrace, seeking solace in the warmth of her presence as my tears cascaded down onto her soft shoulder. I felt like a child once more, yearning for her soothing touch as she lovingly caressed my head and back.

"It has been nearly three decades since he left us," she spoke as her tender fingertips wiped away my tears with a mother's grace. "He held you dear until the very end and prayed for your well-being."

I sat beside her to see her better. A blend of joy and sorrow revealed a lifetime of dedication etched, etched in the gentle creases of her weathered skin. From her countenance emanated a timeless beauty, suffused with an ethereal glow of love that resided within her.

"How is Howmi, mother?" I inquired, longing for news of my brother.

"He is well, my son," she replied in a comforting voice, "He resides nearby, living happily with his wife and three children."

"Praise be to God. Has he been good to you?"

"Yes, my dear," she responded with a gentle smile. "He has matured and evolved in many ways. Though he faces challenges like everyone else, he perseveres with determination and resilience."

"Oh, mother, how I have yearned for you all these years," I confessed.

"Yes, my dear," her reassuring voice conveyed a deep understanding that mirrored my own emotions.

"It feels like a dream, having you here, my son, tangible and real," she whispered through tears of joy.

We wept together, our eyes locked in a gaze of disbelief as if trying to comprehend the reality of our long-awaited reunion.

"Would you like to meet my family now?" I inquired gently.

"Oh, yes, that would be delightful, my son," her voice quivered with excitement as she wiped her tears off.

"It will take a while to introduce everyone. Are you ready, mother?"

"Yes, I wish to meet them now, my son. Do I look presentable?" she asked, adjusting the braid cascading over her right shoulder.

"Yes, mother. You are beautiful, as ever. You look gorgeous," I assured her, our smiles signaling our readiness.

All my family members had gathered, assembling in front of mother's headquarters Hall, where she had hosted countless events and counseled crowds of visitors for years.

Sensing her difficulty in projecting her welcome, I

took the initiative to address the gathering, "Dear ones, Grandma Pari extends her heartfelt welcome to each and every one of you! She is truly excited to meet all of you. Please, come forward one by one to greet her."

As I surveyed the lively scene, I spotted Negawr seated nearby on a bench beside Farah, with PawkZawd standing by her side, holding her hand.

"Mother, look over there. Do you recognize Negawr? That's my wife," I pointed out with pride.

"Oh, dearest Negawr," she exclaimed, waving her hand excitedly.

"And the boy she is holding hands with is Pawkzawd, my youngest son."

"How wonderful. She is just as lovely as she was when she was a little girl, and your son, he looks like an angel," as she signaled, beckoning them to come.

Amidst the joyful chatter and excitement, Negawr walked hand in hand with Pawkzawd up the stairs.

Mother struggled to stand up as I rushed to help her, "please don't exert yourself, mother. They will come to you,"

"I can manage, my son," she insisted as she rose to her feet.

"Welcome, my dear Negawr! Oh, it is wonderful to have you here," she exclaimed with open arms, eager to embrace her.

"Mother! My dearest Aunt Pari, I am truly honored to be here with you," Negawr expressed warmly as they embraced each other for a long moment. Then, she knelt with reverence and kissed mother's hand before introducing Pawkzawd.

Mother watched him in wonder as he reached out his hand to shake hers. Unable to resist any longer, she pulled him up to the seat next to her with some effort as I jumped in to assist. She then seated him on her lap, holding him tight and tenderly kissing and caressing him.

"Praise be to God. Bless your heart, my Pawkzawd, my grandson. You are light to my eyes, such a special boy, you are an angel! God bless you," she continued, brimming with joy and affection as tears of happiness flowed down her cheeks.

Negawr stepped aside to open the way for others who had come up the stairs as they entered.

Mother kissed Pawkzawd and allowed him to sit by her side to attend to the arriving family members.

"My dearest Behzawd, would you please make our

loved ones comfortable? Oh, this is a wonderful day," she expressed with joy.

"Yes, mother. Don't worry,"

One by one, they came in.

"Hello, Grandma Pari, my name is Mina."

"Mina is my wife and the mother of our four sons," I explained.

"Welcome, Mina, dear. It is so gracious of you to be part of the family,"

I expanded on their relations with me as everyone introduced themselves. Mother was joyful, her eyes lighting up with each new introduction, hardly able to take her eyes off one person before the next was introduced.

"Welcome home, my dear. I am so happy you are here. Praise God," she greeted everyone.

She blessed each person with a gesture of her hand over their head as much as she could reach, whispering prayers as they kissed her free hand.

The blessed ones then walked over to the side and took a place in the room. The procession came to an end, with the last one being blessed. Everyone had taken a place and settled in their own selected spot, an alcove, sitting on a bench, or standing around facing mother.

I sat by my mother's side on the same bench while Negawr and Pawkzawd were seated on a bench to my right. Mother looked around in disbelief.

"My dear ones, this is the most memorable day of my life. It is hard to contain all this happiness at once. I hope you feel at home in Mihan."

Farah, who had disappeared since Negawr came to meet mother, came in and whispered in my ears: "There are 19 guesthouses available right now. Do you think it is enough for the families?"

I quickly made some family counts; "10, 11, 12… Yes, dear, it should be enough."

"Would you like to choose specific guesthouses for everyone?" she asked, referring to the village guesthouses typically used to accommodate trade caravans as they passed through.

"What would be easiest? This must be quite an inconvenience."

"Oh, not at all, my dearest Behzawd, there is no need for concern. I simply want to know about your preferences."

"Can I help?"

"When you are ready, kindly furnish me with the count of family members for each household, and I shall take care of the rest."

"Thank you, my dearest. You are the kindred spirit I have long yearned for, my sweet sister."

"You stay with Mother. I will guide each family to their individual abode once I have their counts."

In that instant, a man entered, his visage strikingly familiar. It suddenly dawned on me that he was my twin brother. With a rush of emotions, I hurried to embrace him.

"Is it truly you, Howmi? Oh, dear brother, how I have missed you."

After our initial embrace, we locked eyes, then enfolded each other once more, going through several rounds of disbelief.

"Welcome home, brother! What an honor."

"The honor is entirely mine. Let me look at you, Howmi. Oh, my goodness, I cannot remember, but we shared that confined space in the womb," we chuckled. Our eyes conveyed more than our words ever could. A peculiar bond with the past evoked both bittersweet and joyful tunes in my heart as I held him dear.

He then turned his curious gaze towards the room filled with my family, placing a hand over his heart and bowed: "Peace! Welcome!"

"This is my only brother, Howmi," I declared.

"Peace be upon you, dear uncle," the heartfelt greeting echoed from all around.

Eager to ease Howmi's shyness, "I will introduce you to everyone when they are leaving, my brother." I assured him.

Turning to the assembled guests, I continued, "Aunt Farah has graciously arranged accommodation for your stay. When you are ready, please step forward so she can show you to your places," I added, placing my arm around her shoulder. " God Willing, we'll have ample opportunity to celebrate and reconnect. Who would like to go first?"

Puyaw, who happened to be closest to the exit, volunteered, as he had lingered behind to ensure everyone's safe arrival. He warmly shook hands with Howmi as I introduced him, then gallantly kissed mother's hand. Farah embraced him in a heartfelt hug, reciprocated warmly. His wife and children followed suit, exchanging greetings as they left the room.

As the night descended and everyone settled into their respective accommodations, Howmi rose, signaling his departure.

"Would you like to come and stay with my family?" he kindly offered.

"Oh, thank you, brother," I responded. "Let me spend some time catching up with mother first. I would be delighted to visit your family soon."

"We will come to see you tomorrow, God Willing. Rest well, brother."

"We shall, thank you, Howmi."

"I am truly happy to see you Behzawd,"

"Yes, me too, my brother. God Bliss you," I replied, a sense of peace washing over me as I realized it was the first time I didn't feel threatened while conversing with him.

Mother happily watched us with joy, still in disbelief.

Farah returned, informing us that everyone was settled and dinner had been served in each guest's residence as we conversed. As I watched her, I noticed her striking similarities with our mother in her thoughtful demeaner and meticulous caring for everyone but herself.

Upon seeing Pawkzawd, who had fallen asleep in Negawr's arms, Farah hurried to prepare a bed for him while attendants brought in food and set the table.

With Farah's assistance, Negawr gently tucked Pawkzawd into bed before joining us at the dining table. Negawr took a seat to my right while Farah sat to my left, and I cherished the sight of mother seated across from me. The cozy group we formed was one of a kind, as we came together to share my first meal with mother and Farah after sixty years of separation.

Mother's face radiated with happiness, and her eyes glistened with joyful tears each time our gazes met. The scene before me was nothing short of heavenly — a tranquil and surreal setting, surrounded by the presence of three earthly angels who graced my life.

Chapter 39 The Sorcerer

As I settled into life in Mihan, I soon uncovered the unsettling truth that a sorcerer had entrenched himself in the town, practicing witchcraft since his arrival a few years prior. Under the guise of a healer, he had ensnared the local populace, exploiting the absence of authority following my father's passing. Superstition was woven into the fabric of the community in the shadow of their deep-seated fears and uncertainties.

The sorcerer's dark arts had blossomed into a thriving enterprise in the vacuum left by the absence of divine guidance. He had taken on several apprentices from the locals, perpetuating fear and deception on a grand scale.

Amidst this turmoil, a palpable absence of tranquility and empathy hung over society, eroding peace and compassion in every interaction.

The lack of Divine presence had allowed malevolent forces to run rampant, afflicting people of all ages. From the moment I set foot back in Mihan, I felt compelled to share the teachings of scripture, drawing from the wisdom imparted by my late Uncle Kia.

My sermons aroused the ire of the sorcerer, who turned his dark sorcery towards me, my family, and anyone associated with me. As he sought to solidify his grip on power, his malevolent actions escalated, unleashing chaos and instilling a pervasive sense of dread among the vulnerable populace.

While spreading the Word of God, I offered counsel to those in search of spiritual enlightenment, reminding them of the boundless potential within each soul to reach heavenly heights. I warned against the allure of sorcery, which shackles the spirit with malevolence and leads to despair.

The sorcerer's apprentice sought to disrupt my sermons, harassing individuals with pranks and deceitful prophecies to undermine my teachings.

Armed with unwavering faith and the Sword of the Divine Word, I stood firm against their attacks, in public and in private, urging repentance and embracing goodness for prosperity.

"O my people, within each of you resides a soul bestowed with the boundless potential to ascend to the very heights of the heavens. Your Creator, the Sustainer of your existence, is the One God who Watch over you. Should your heart yearn for true prosperity and the bliss of divine communion, heed the divine guidance set forth for you. Your spirit was crafted to be free, a gift from the Divine. Only through His grace can your sorrows be lifted and replaced with boundless joy …

"Beware of the allure of sorcery, for it shackles your soul with malevolence, tarnishing your spirit and burdening you with remorse and anguish. It is a deceptive illusion, promising fulfillment yet leading only to an abyss of desolation from which escape seems impossible, plunging you into the depths of despair ..."

I extended an olive branch to the sorcerer, offering him the choice to join me in peace or leave the town. Despite my pleas for peace, the sorcerer and his followers remained defiant, spreading fear and discord wherever they found the opportunity, casting a looming shadow over the town.

His apprentices insidiously infiltrated my sermons, causing disruptions and tormenting individuals with pranks, mockery, and deceitful prophecies in a bid to undermine my teachings.

"Who is this God of yours, Behzawd? Are you attempting to blend our deities into one? It seems as though you have succumbed to our gods," they jeered, their words dripping with malice. "Leave our land, or we shall drive you out forcefully or pelt you with stones until your last breath fades..."

Standing steadfast as a beacon of light amid the encroaching darkness, I implored all to shun wickedness and embrace the path of Truth and righteousness.

"Fear the Almighty God, the Creator of you and me. Your gods are mere constructs of your own making. This sacred land bears witness to the legacy of my ancestors, who worshipped only One God. They entrusted this land to those who walk the path of Truth. Do not disturb the peace of its inhabitants. Repent and turn to the Most Forgiving, Most Merciful God. If you forsake mischief, you may find solace here. Otherwise, depart in peace."

Alas, the gang remained obstinate, persisting in their malevolent schemes as their presence exuded hostility and chaos, brazenly intruding wherever they pleased, sowing seeds of doubt and falsehood among the unsuspecting populace.

Fear, distrust, animosity, and discord permeated the social fabric, casting a foreboding shadow over every aspect of life. The pernicious influence of their malevolence spared no one, leaving behind a wake of shattered lives and fractured spirits.

Chapter 40 Residing In Mihan

To accommodate the influx of new residents I had brought to Mihan, my adult sons embarked on a series of construction projects. Each diligently built a new home within the village complex situated to the east of my ancestral home. Many individuals who remained steadfast in upholding my father's teachings willingly offered their assistance.

In just under two years, the construction of their homes was completed, and every member of the family settled into their own abode in Mihan. The meticulous planning ensured that all dwellings were interconnected, enhancing the overall sense of comfort and unity.

Mina and her two children settled nearby to the west of Mother's residence. Negawr, PawkZawd, and I resided in our own home nestled between the Farah's and Mother's residences. Farah devoted much of her time to fulfilling her village-wide responsibilities or caring for Mother, rarely finding time to spend in her own house.

My family spent the evenings in the company of mother, fostering a deep bond between her and Negawr, while PawkZawd entertained everyone with his amusing curiosity.

As Farah and I grew closer, her relentless dedication and hard work sparked concern within me. It appeared as though she had shouldered all the responsibilities that once belonged to our late father, striving to maintain unity not just at home but among the entire city.

One evening, as we sat together in contemplative silence, I mustered the courage to broach a sensitive topic. "Sis, have you ever pondered the idea of marriage?"

With a wistful look in her eyes, Farah delved into memories of her past. "Yes, once I was wed to one of Father's most trusted aides when I reached the age of sixteen," her tone tinged with a hint of melancholy. "He was a man of remarkable character. However, after our fifth anniversary, he inexplicably fell ill and departed from this world within a mere span of months. The cause of his sudden ailment remains a haunting mystery that lingers in my heart to this day."

"Oh, my dear little sister, please forgive me for not being there for you," as I truly regretted the fact that I was not there to comfort her when she needed me.

"O, my beloved brother, Behzawd, just knowing that a soul as kind and caring as yours exists in this world was enough to sustain my hope for brighter days like these," she responded with her usual warmth and gratitude.

"Why did you choose not to remarry, Sis?" I gently inquired.

"It is hard to explain, my dearest. He left a void that no other man could fill. May God bless their souls. I felt compelled then to step into the shoes of our late Father's trusted aide. The privilege of being his wife remains the pinnacle of honor in my life," she reflected with a sense of nostalgia.

"Indeed, safeguarding his legacy amidst the tumultuous sea of challenges has proven to be a daunting task, as you shall discover in time," she continued with determination.

"I am certain you have excelled in upholding his legacy, dear sister. Your dedication is commendable," I praised her wholeheartedly. " May I humbly ask if you would now entrust me with your confidence and allow yourself the well-deserved respite you so earnestly need?"

"O, thank you, dearest brother. I cannot fathom placing my trust in anyone else but you,"

"Let us collaborate on a plan to allocate and

delegate tasks among my sons, ensuring all responsibilities are managed under your expert guidance until you are ready to relinquish control and embrace a life free from worries."

"Oh, Behzawd, God favored me the precious gift of having you as a role model in my youth, and in your absence, I turned to our parents for guidance. So, I stand strong today, willing to face any challenge with you by my side. If so, please God."

"Praise be to God. Yes, indeed, your strength and wisdom shine brightly, but even the strongest need respite. You can now place your trust in my sons with confidence, assured that they will fulfill their duties diligently. Simply guide them in comprehending their roles, and then allow them to take the lead."

Farah seized the opportunity, allocating tasks based on each individual's strengths and abilities. Before long, all ten of my sons had honed their skills in managing Mihan's affairs, easing Farah's burden significantly.

With her lightened workload, Farah could devote more time to caring for our mother and Pawkzawd, who cherished the moments spent with grandma Pari.

On his fourth birthday, following a grand family celebration, PawkZawd caught me and Negawr by surprise.

"Can I request a special birthday present?" he inquired.

"Sure, my son, what do you have in mind?" I responded.

"Can I sleep in the same room as Aunt Farah? That way, I can be close to Grandma Pari, too," he proposed with excitement.

Negawr wrestled with the idea of being separated from him for the night.

"But I will feel sad without you, PawkZawd!" she expressed.

"You can stay too, mommy," was his solution.

"Sweetheart, who will wake Daddy up in the morning?"

"Oh, okay, you go with Daddy,"

We laughed. When she eventually gave in to his request, he leaped into her arms for an extended hug.

"I have to save this for the whole night," he declared, attempting to preserve the embrace.

We chuckled as we watched him trying to sustain

the hug within his crossed arms, playfully renewing it while we were present.

PawkZawd began to spend more time with Mother and Farah, taking advantage of the additional free time Farah now had at her disposal.

However, a few weeks later, Mother's health took a sudden turn for the worse, deteriorating rapidly despite the doctors' best efforts. Sadly, her condition continued to decline with no chance of recovery. She peacefully passed away in her sleep within a month.

Mother's passing deeply affected PawkZawd emotionally. Despite being shielded from many of the details, he struggled to comprehend why he could no longer be with his grandmother. His bond with Farah grew even stronger as Farah made extra efforts to bring him joy. Whether they were together at "grandma Pari's" or Farah was with us, everyone made a conscious effort to lessen the impact of Grandma's absence on PawkZawd.

Chapter 41 Departure on Arrival

The sorcerer was resolute in his efforts to salvage his business and retain his followers, even resorting to schemes to drive me away from Mihan. There was an unmistakable malevolence in the dark spells he unleashed. The subsequent series of calamities, mysterious illnesses, and deaths that befell the village were no mere coincidences. Yet, these events shaped me into the person I needed to become.

Three months after my mother's passing, Negawr suddenly fell ill at the dinner table. I rushed to fetch the doctor while Farah assisted her in lying down. After examining Negawr, the doctor requested a private conversation with me:

"I have some wonderful news for you, Behzawd. Your wife is expecting a baby."

"Oh, Praise be to God! What a miraculous blessing," I exclaimed in joy.

"But I must warn you that her condition is extremely dangerous. Given her chronic anemia, it is imperative that she rests adequately, maintains a healthy diet, and avoids stress to ensure a successful pregnancy."

"Understood. I will ensure that she receives excellent care and tranquility."

After the doctor left, Farah and I deliberated on the situation and agreed that Pawkzawd should spend more time with Farah to allow Negawr to rest.

In a matter of months, the situation worsened as Negawr's body succumbed to a mysterious illness, resulting in rapid weight loss and rendering her unable to walk unassisted. As the baby continued to grow inside her, her health further declined. Mina remained steadfast by her side, providing care and support day and night.

Pawkzawd was overjoyed by the prospect of welcoming a younger sibling soon, which helped him cope with the time limit with his mother. He visited her multiple times a day for a short period of time, striving to show strength in her presence. Together, they shared moments of laughter as he uplifted her spirits.

"Oh, the fruit of my love, Pawkzawd, why do you look troubled? I will recover soon, once our baby arrives and is in your arms... praise be to God," as she reassured him tenderly.

Pawkzawd held onto her arm with apparent concern. "I will stay by your side, mother. I want to be here with you a little longer. Are you feeling any pain?" he inquired, his worry evident in his voice.

"No, my dear one, I am not in pain at all. I just need to be very cautious now, but I will regain my strength soon," Negawr reassured him with a smile, aiming to alleviate his stress.

As Pawkzawd left, Negawr could not help but cry, the memory of his sad face and teary eyes haunting her, the ache of not being able to hold him in her arms piercing her heart.

Despite the finest medical experts at her disposal, every breath seemed to drain life out of her body. Helpless, I remained by her side, day and night, offering prayers and anything I could do to make her more comfortable. It felt like a never-ending nightmare, a torment I prayed would dissipate once she gave birth.

Approaching the scheduled delivery time, an internal doctor, a midwife, and their skilled team provided round-the-clock care in eager anticipation of the baby's arrival.

As Negawr went into labor, her blood pressure plummeted to dangerous levels. Her heartbeat was erratic, and she lacked the strength to push.

I held her hand tightly, offering words of

encouragement as she struggled through contractions. "You're doing great, my dear. Take a deep breath..."

"Darling, please take care of our children," she whispered.

"We will take care of them together, my love. Don't worry, let's focus on your breathing..."

Near the sunset, the midwife gently urged me to step outside for a break and return later.

"But I have to be here with her," I insisted.

"It would help you more if you took a short break, Sir Behzawd," she advised.

Reluctant, I complied and ventured outside. The twilight sky enveloped the surroundings in a deep, enigmatic hue as I strolled back and forth in the garden beneath Negawr's chamber, the sound of my heartbeat echoing in the quiet.

After a few minutes, unable to bear the separation any longer, I hastened back to her bedside. The doctor was frantically engaged in his efforts to revive her, with the vigilant midwife standing nearby.

Mina was holding a bundle, which she tried to show me when I passed her on my way to Negawr.

"Sir Behzawd, your son is safe and healthy. Look,"

Mina whispered to catch my attention.

I approached Negawr. Her eyes were shut. Her once radiant face bore a bluish hue as if the very light of her life had faded. Sitting beside her, I took her hand in mine, gently caressing her head. The doctor, positioned on the opposite side of the bed, rose and moved aside.

"Oh, my beloved Negawr, you must stay strong. Our son is healthy," I murmured softly, hoping my words would infuse her with the fortitude to battle on.

Her eyes fluttered open, meeting mine for a fleeting moment. A soft smile graced her lips as she squeezed my hand gently before her eyes closed again. With effort, she placed her hand first on my eyes, then on my lips. I felt her grasp slacken as I looked around in search of assistance with a sense of urgency.

The doctor shook his hopeless head slowly from side to side.

"Oh, no! My dearest, please don't leave me,"

I cradled her lifeless form in my arms, my tears cascading onto her once vibrant countenance as I mourned.

"Oh, Lord, she was truly one of Your angels. Thank You, Lord, for the precious gift of her presence.

Grant me the strength to endure this loss and guide me in nurturing her children to walk in Your straight path. May them be steadfast in faith, resilient in their sorrow, and unwavering in their belief in You, just as she was. Surely, she was among Your noblest servants, and now, Your celestial hosts rejoice in her flight to Your embrace. All praise and gratitude belong to You, my Lord, for blessing me with her companionship. She will be part of me. Help me to endure this separation, Oh, my dear Lord..."

A heart wrenching agony gripped my soul, compelling my prayers that echoed in mournful lamentations. As others tried to lead me away, I implored them to leave me with her in solitude.

Time lost its meaning as I silent myself by her side until a baby's cry pierced the air.

Mina, holding the infant in her arms, stood near the doorway. Drawing closer, she spoke softly, "He is a beautiful boy, dearest! Would you like to hold him?"

With tender care, I laid Negawr down gently, wiped away my tears, and opened my arms to embrace the new life, a final gift that she had left me before her departure.

As soon as I received the baby, he ceased to cry, gazing directly at me with his large, dark eyes.

"Blessed is Thy Name, Lord. Grant me the strength to nurture this precious gift she has left behind. Blessed is the One above who has ordained this little angel to carry forward her light in this world..."

"I found myself overflowing with praises for The Only One Whose Divine Presence permeated all things. "Truly, this baby is a sight to behold! Blessed be Your Name, ..., He shall uphold what pleases You, my Lord. I shall name him Nimaw," I declared.

"What a fitting choice of name, Sir Behzawd, Just and Equitable in all matters! Under your guidance, he will surely embody the truth of his name. May God grant it so," Mina affirmed in agreement.

Nimaw, my twelfth son, was the only child born to me in Mihan, a radiant blessing amidst the veils of profound grief.

With Negawr removed from the picture, the sinister intentions of the sorcerer posed a looming threat to our two young sons she had left me. As I sought to shield them from harm, a growing chasm emerged, separating me from the outside world.

My older sons had blossomed into adults, capable of tending to their own lives and engrossed in the joys of raising their own children.

Little did I know that the envious whisperer sought an opening within the circle of my most trusted ones. My unwavering focus on my younger children inadvertently nurtured toxic thoughts that clouded the awareness of my ten elder sons—a volatile concoction primed to ignite with a mere spark. A gathering storm, ready to unleash yet another potentially devastating blow upon our grieving family.

Chapter 42 New Routines

The loss of Negawr left a profound void within my family, touching each member in a unique and poignant way. Despite her memories that pierced my heart like a sharp blade, I understood the importance of fulfilling my duty to raise our two young ones and safeguard my people from the treacherous traps laid by the sorcerer.

Embodying unique facets of Negawr's character, Pawkzawd, and Nimaw necessitated protection not only from the internal emotional reverberations of her absence but also from the perilous shadows of the sorcerer's realm.

While Mina devoted herself to overseeing our household affairs and nurturing my young ones, I fulfilled my duties within our home and across the village.

With meticulous care, I selected skilled mentors to be overseen by Farah, tasked with guiding Pawkzawd, whose insatiable thirst for knowledge spanned the realms of science, sports, and the arts.

Meanwhile, little Nimaw's world continued to unfold under Mina's nurturing watch, cradled in the arms of a motherly caregiver, Nanny, who had recently endured the sorrow of losing her own newborn child.

True to his routine, Pawkzawd would rise early each morning, his excitement palpable at the thought of seeing Aunt Farah. Grasping his beloved bag, a constant companion, he would eagerly position himself by the doorway, ready to embark on the day's adventures.

"Father, we're running late. Aunt Farah is waiting," he would exclaim.

"Yes, my son, I'm on my way. Would you not care for a quick breakfast with me?"

"Oh, no, father, Aunt Farah has already set the table," he assured me.

Hand in hand, we strolled across the yard to Farah's abode, where my late parents once resided.

Like a devoted mother awaiting her child, Farah greeted Pawkzawd each morning with unwavering anticipation. She served as his dearest confidante, mentor, and vigilant overseer, guiding his mentors throughout the day.

After wrapping up my daily affairs in town, I made my way to Farah's place, where the three of us then walked over to my home. Dinner awaited us as we gathered, joined by Mina, Nanny, and little Nimaw.

Later, the evening unfolded with an abundance of conversation, laughter, and playful moments. When Nimaw succumbed to sleep, Pawkzawd assumed the role of a protective big brother, hushing to ensure a peaceful environment to guard his brother's sleep.

"Father, may we accompany Aunt Farah back home?" Pawkzawd inquired, seeking to prolong the evening and cherish his moments with her

"Yes, my son. She must be tired,"

As we reached Farah's doorstep, Pawkzawd wrapped her in a lingering embrace.

"Thank you, Aunt Farah. I love you," he would whisper.

"I love you too, my sweetheart. Oh, how I wish you could stay. Promise me you'll return early in the morning," she pleaded with affection and longing.

"I promise Aunt Farah,"

"Sweet dreams, my love,"

"Sweet dreams, Aunt Farah,"

In the quiet passage of time, Farah realized the significance of Pawkzawd returning each night to the solace of his own bed. A ritual that whispered peace to my heart, yearning and restless in his absence.

Farah had become the critical thread that wove through the fabric of Pawkzawd's world, bridging across the chasm of his emotional void. In her presence, the gentle balm of comfort and loving care mended the fractures left by the absence of his beloved mother.

Pawkzawd, in his silent reverie, embraced his grieving ache in a healing process with a gradual unfolding, like petals unfurling at dawn's first light.

Chapter 43 The Curious Boy

A bout to turn eighty, I found myself embarking on a new journey of discovery alongside two inquisitive boys who captivated all my attention. Pawkzawd's presence exuded a radiant warmth of pure affection, drawing all towards him for at least a tender embrace. His unwavering fascination for nature, the mysteries of the universe, and the intricate dance of the cosmos forged a unique connection between us that transcended a normal father and son relationship.

In the midst of my focused parenting, recollections of Negawr's practical teachings challenged me to understand the essence of *"selfless love that can unveil the hidden pathways to genuine happiness."*

Each day, as we strolled to and from Farah's, our conversations meandered through the realms of Pawkzawd's boundless curiosity. From the majestic ascent of the morning sun to the ethereal symphony of birds in graceful flight or from the glittering expanse of stars adorning the night sky to the serene gaze of the moon, our dialogues traversed the marvels of the world, stretching into the late hours of the night until he fell asleep.

"Father, have you ever counted the stars?"

"No, my son. Have you?"

"No, there are so many, my eyes grow weary, and my vision blurs when I try to count them,"

"Indeed, my dear one, the stars in the heavens surpass our capacity for enumeration or even comprehension. They exist beyond the reach of our limited sight,"

"Oh, Father, I yearn to know more, please, enlighten me,"

"My beloved, to God belongs the Kingdom of this vast and ever-expanding universe. The armies of the heavens and the earth are constantly working to carry out His Divine Will. Every creation, no matter how minuscule – as tiny as a mustard seed nestled in the soil – is meticulously recorded in His infinite knowledge. Through His Divine Decree, the mere thought of anything transforms into a reality. When He Intends for a thing to be, it is …"

"Father, how can I draw near to Him? Can I seek His presence as I do with you?"

"My son, He is nearer to you than I could ever be. Can you sense this?" I took his little hand and placed his finger on the pulsing vein in his neck, guiding him to feel the rhythmic beat beneath his touch. Gradually, his eyes widened in awe as he experienced the palpable sensation of his own heartbeat.

"Do you feel your pulse?"

"Yes, father,"

"He is closer to you than this. His presence resides between your heart, nestled here, and your mind, resting here," as I pointed to his heart and his head. "He knows before you feel or you think,"

"That is awesome, father. If He already knows, why should I speak to Him? Why should I need to pray to Him?"

"Ah, my dear one, just like when you request something of me, it makes you feel closer to me when your wish is fulfilled. Your prayers help you get closer to your understanding of His Grace. The closer you feel to Him by seeking Him, living in His divine Presence, and trusting Him as your sole Provider, the more you draw nearer to Him. He is The Strongest protection and The Mightiest friend when you surrender your will, completely, to His Will, when you turn to Him alone in times of joy and sorrow,"

"How do I know if I have truly surrendered my will to Him? When will I be in His presence?"

"He, Himself, will be your Guide, my son. His Perception encompasses all, from whispered thoughts to unspoken desires, for nothing is concealed from His omniscience. He Hears and Sees everything. Just as He comprehends the depths of our hearts, He also fathoms the unfathomable depths of the oceans and the cosmos. When you consecrate your heart as a sanctuary solely for Him, inviting His presence to dwell within you, He will illuminate your path with a shining light in your heart, which becomes the wisdom by which you are guided to walk in The Straight Path. At that point, you become mindful of each breath as you take strides with the sole intent of drawing closer to Him."

Pawkzawd listened with his eyes, asking for more.

"Consider this: if our hearts are occupied with affections for other than Him, they become the distractions like veils by which our focus is diverted from Him. In doing so, we inadvertently create a chasm between ourselves and our Beloved. That is different than if our love for others was rooted in our love for Him and His boundless Love for all His creation,"

"Father, can I ever behold Him?"

"My son, can you look into the sun?"

"No, it hurts my eyes,"

"Yes, it could blind you if you did,"

"Can you look into the sun, father?"

"No, my dear, it would blind me also. How can we, with our limited capacity and consciousness, aspire to grasp His infinite nature and who has fashioned countless suns?"

"Don't know, father!"

Consider this - Can the fish perceive the water that surrounds them?"

"Well, the fish can sense it, glide through it, its sight lies within the water that it can see, well, can it see, father?"

"Can we see the air we breathe?"

"Well, it envelops us. It is everywhere," as he was thinking hard, "we breathe it into our lungs, but we cannot see it,"

"Indeed, my son, we are finite beings, bound within an infinite expanse in every aspect. Our understanding is confined to what we can perceive."

"Does that mean I can never behold God?"

"With our physical eyes, you cannot, my son, but through your spirit, when and if you are granted access to higher realms of enlightenment that enable you to see Him everywhere,"

"Who should grant access, father?"

"Only God, my son,"

"Can I petition Him for access?"

"Yes, by following His divine laws. He created every one of us in the nature of His Knowledge by which we intuitively distinguish truth from falsehood if we are mindful. He has made His laws clearly known through His messengers who demonstrated His message through their own lives and explained right from wrong."

"How Does He Know, father?"

"Can you think of a little chip they put in computers these days? I think, ummmm…, they call it CPU?"

"Is CPU the brain or heart of the computer?"

"I am not sure if computers have a heart, but they definitely must have a brain. But there is a difference between the two, my son! The human brain is like a computer chip with a divine circuit that regulates our perception of the world and, therefore, the development of our senses. When we succeed in synchronizing the brain and the heart of our divine circuit, the auto-circuit of the divine laws may grant us access to transcend up into higher realms of the Divine Spirit."

"Can I learn all of the Divine Laws, father?"

"Yes, my son. It is a life-long process of purified intention in seeking and application of His Word, as delivered by His messengers and preserved in the holy scriptures."

"Are all holy scriptures His Pure Word, father? How can we be certain that they are not tainted by human hands, father?"

Pawkzawd's quest for knowledge was intertwined with struggles to comprehend the limitations of human existence. At times, I was left with wonders myself as I reflected on the reverberations of my elders' wisdom within the depths of my own youthful heart.

"I feel I know nothing, Father. I must study more," he often admitted with genuine concern.

"Be patient, my son," I tried to calm his restless spirit. "At seven, you stand on good ground, poised for a lifetime brimming with revelations. I perceive in you the seeds of a noble spirit, destined to safeguard the sanctity of your being to serve higher purposes."

"How do you know, father?"

"You possess a curious spirit, a seeker's heart, and above all, you are eager to behold Him," I explained. "In your pursuit, you shall encounter His Presence. It is easy to remember that He resides within you, nearer to you than your own self, nestled between your heart and your mind."

In such moments, the mysteries of the universe whispered secrets into my very soul as my own new discovery.

Thus, we journeyed onward together along the path of enlightenment with spirits intertwined in a dance of exploration and revelation, bound by a strengthened thread of faith.

Chapter 44 A Lesson

Pawkzawd, at the tender age of seven, shared an unbreakable bond with his two-year-old brother, Nimaw. Farah, who was entrusted with Pawkzawd's care, poured her heart and soul into nurturing him as if his well-being were the very essence of her existence. Every moment was carefully crafted by Farah to instill seeds of knowledge and character-building wisdom. Their bond was so strong that Pawkzawd's longing for his mother slowly dissipated into the background.

In the face of fleeting moments of longing, Farah masterfully shielded him from any emotional turbulence through whimsical and creative activities, ensuring that each day was filled with joyful development.

Farah's devotion knew no bounds as she tended to Pawkzawd tirelessly, prompting me to intervene out of concern for her own well-being. "Dear Farah, caring for Pawkzawd demands so much of you. You must remember to take care of yourself and allow yourself some rest," I urged her on multiple occasions.

"My dear brother," she would reply from the bottom of her heart. "He is not a burden to me; he is the very light of my life."

One fateful day, as I dropped off Pawkzawd, Farah's demeanor took me by surprise as she addressed me with unwavering resolve. "We should not come for dinner tonight, my dear brother, and for a few days until Pawkzawd learns an important lesson," she declared solemnly.

Perplexed, I inquired, "What kind of lesson, Farah? And what does it have to do with dinner?"

"He needs some time to reflect and acknowledge the mistake he has made,"

"Wrong? Pawkzawd?" I questioned, exchanging a puzzled glance with Pawkzawd, who was equally confused.

Turning to Pawkzawd, I asked gently, "Do you know what mistake you have made, my son?"

He shook his head from side to side. "No, father. What did I do, Aunt Farah? I am sorry!"

"Well, I hope I am wrong, my dear, but let us check your bag first," Farah replied.

Pawkzawd handed his bag to her. She knelt down and emptied the contents onto the floor as she spoke.

"I have searched everywhere for our late father's

Redaw. A few days ago, I left it on the table to remind myself to give it to you. But it's no longer there."

At this moment, she pulled the Redaw out of the bag. The last time I had laid eyes on that beautifully handcrafted green cloth was on my father's shoulders before I departed from home over sixty-five years ago. I recalled how regal he appeared, resembling a king as he wore it to formal gatherings.

"Ah. Here it is! My dear, did you put this in your bag?" as she lifted the Redaw to show him.

Pawkzawd was visibly distraught, tears streaming down his cheeks. "No, Aunty, I didn't take it. I don't remember," he replied with genuine sorrow.

"Well, perhaps today you will be working on a lesson to stay with you for the rest of your life. Would you mind?" her heavy words hung in the air.

"Okay, Aunty."

"What do you think would be a suitable consequence for this?" She inquired.

"I am not sure, Aunty,"

Farah turned to me with glistening eyes filled with tears, whispering, "I believe it's crucial for Pawkzawd to remember this. Don't you agree, brother?"

"Yes, you are absolutely right," I concurred, my unease lingering over the entire ordeal.

"Would you agree he should stay here for a week to reflect on this lesson?" she continued, shaking the Redaw to smooth out its wrinkles.

"Father Farshawd, may peace be upon his soul, left this for you before he passed," she said, offering the Redaw to me.

"God bless his soul," I murmured, envisioning his gentle face in my mind as I accepted the Redaw on my arm.

By accepting the Redaw, I felt the weight of a solemn mission settling on my shoulders. This anointed, handcrafted strip of cloth transcended its material form, embodying a profound significance as a symbol of holiness, a shield against malevolence, and a bestower of divine authority upon its wearer.

Passed down through generations, the Redaw was a tangible link to the revered holy figure entrusted from father to chosen son to carry on a spiritual legacy within a prophetic lineage. As I embraced my role as a bridge between the past and the future, I bore the weight of tradition and the promise of divine guidance with reverence and humility.

I wiped away my tears and sat on the ground, meeting Pawkzawd's teary eyes. I lifted him up and cradled him on my lap. "Do you know why you took this, my son?" I inquired softly.

"No, I did not,"

"I trust you, my son. Perhaps it got mixed up with your belongings as you were preparing to return home,"

"Maybe, I don't know, father,"

"Whatever happened is in the past. As human beings, we bear responsibility for our actions, which entail consequences if we lack vigilance. Do you remember your yearning to draw closer to God?" I reminded him.

"Yes, father,"

"At times, these consequences are essential to guide us on our journey and help us reach our spiritual aspirations with a pure heart. Let us do as Aunt Farah suggests. You shall stay here for a week, and I will visit you every day. This will serve as your valuable lesson of the week. Would you agree?"

"Yes, Father, would you promise to visit me? I will die without you,"

"Oh, my dear, you won't die." I chuckled to lighten his stress. "I promise to visit you every day. Can you help Aunt Farah with her chores around here as the man of the house?"

"Yes, father. I will help her like a big man,"

"You make a great big man, my son," I embraced him tight while we laughed.

As I turned to leave to begin my busy day, he called out, "Come back soon, father."

"I shall, my son, God Willing,"

Throughout the day and indeed the entire week, a lingering sense of unease gnawed at me as I contemplated the situation. Despite my unwavering belief in Pawkzawd's innocence, I recognized the potential for this seemingly harsh punishment to impart a valuable lesson to him.

Observing Farah and Pawkzawd throughout the week, witnessing their bond and mutual support grow stronger, brought me a deep sense of peace in knowing that they both found solace in this shared experience within a safe and loving environment.

Every evening, I made a brief visit before heading home, filled with joy from the sound of their shared laughter. As the agreed-upon week drew to a close, I felt a sense of contentment, knowing that we would soon be walking home together again.

Trying to stifle their giggle upon my arrival, after greetings exchanges, Farah asked, "Would you not be upset, brother, if Pawkzawd were to tell you the truth?"

"Of course not, sister, I value the truth anytime,"

Farah encouraged Pawkzawd: "Go ahead, dear, tell your father about our secret,"

"Oh no, Aunty, you tell him,"

"No, you can do it,"

"But I don't know where to start," Pawkzawd confessed.

They exchanged supportive glances and smiles as I observed in amused confusion.

"Okay, I will tell him. Would you hold my hand for strength?" Their interaction revealed a deep level of trust and a genuinely mutually happy relationship.

Farah sat down on the floor beside Pawkzawd. She first embraced him, then took his hand before speaking.

"I am deeply ashamed, my brother. I confess that I have lied, and all of this was my doing. Pawkzawd spoke the truth. He was unaware of and did not take the Redaw. He is the most honest young man I have ever known. My dearest Behzawd, please forgive me. I have been foolish."

"What do you mean, Farah? It is I who should seek your forgiveness for all the trouble,"

"No, my dearest. I deceived you with my cunning scheme. Knowing you would not approve of Pawkzawd staying with me, I placed the Redaw in his bag, making it appear as though he had taken it without my consent. It was the only way to ensure spending more uninterrupted time with him,"

"Oh, my..." I was stunned by the revelation.

"But I promise you, my dear, Pawkzawd has also learned a valuable lesson. Trust me, brother, he now understands the laws of our land." Farah prompted to justify. "Pawkzawd, would you care to enlighten your father on the law of our land?"

"In our land, the owner has the right to punish any thief of a stolen item until justice is served," Pawkzawd recited with confidence.

"Excellent, my dear, your understanding of our laws is impeccable." I praised him, a pang of guilt creeping in as I realized how much they longed to be together for longer periods.

They awaited my response anxiously, with a mix of worry and anticipation evident on their faces.

"That was a harmless prank, Sister. But please, no more,"

They were both relieved by the burden and happy, lifted by the confession.

"No more tricks, my dearest Behzawd, I promise. Would you be open to the idea of Pawkzawd spending the night with me on occasion?" Farah asked in a hopeful plea.

"Of course, my sweet sister, we can plan for that without any tricks,"

We shared a joyous moment as Pawkzawd leaped into my arms, continuing our conversation all the way home. His experience with the truth and the weight of guilt sparked a newfound diligence in him that I discovered later in his quest to live by truth.

Just as I thought we could not be any closer, we found new ways to draw closer in spirit, which in turn nourished our renewed trust and deepened our happiness. In the wake of that pivotal incident, Pawkzawd began staying overnight at Farah's place every other night, a privilege earned through his dedicated completion of tasks and training routines.

Chapter 45 A Dream

Pawkzawd captivated all with his charm and elegance at the tender age of nearly nine. His kind and compassionate nature mirrored his outward appearance, a sight to behold for all who crossed his path. His innate humility not only endeared him to all but also inspired awe at his Perfect Creator, a testament to His flawless design.

That night, he slumbered peacefully in his bed at home. At the break of dawn, as I sat in quiet contemplation, he came bounding towards me.

"Father, father," calling out as he rubbed his eyes to wake up.

I welcomed him with open arms, enfolding him in a warm embrace as he nestled in my lap. He found a restful spot on my arm for his head as I listened.

"Father, I had a dream,"

"May it bring blessings to your life, my son,"

"Yes, father. I saw the sun and the moon,"

"Praise be to God, for those are wondrous signs of His Mercy," being grateful for a sense of profound gratitude for the divine presence in our lives.

"And I saw eleven stars,"

"Praise be to God,"

"But, father, they all came down and prostrated to me," he uttered with a wonderous urgency.

A jolt crossed my heart as I hushed him with a finger to my lips, urging him to lower his voice.

"Indeed, that is a magnificent dream, my son,"

"What does it mean, father? Why should I be quiet?"

"Your dream will come true in due time, my son, but promise me something, would you?"

"Yes, father," he replied earnestly.

"I want you to keep this dream as our secret. It is like a code between you and God. Do not reveal it to anyone, not even your brothers,"

"A secret? Why, father? Is it a bad dream?"

"No, my son. It is a wonderful dream. Our dreams are sometimes difficult to understand, but they are meaningful. We have to put our trust in The One Who Knows all things. He has ordained a Plan for every one of us,"

"Is His Plan good?"

"Of course. All God's Plans are good, my son. We comprehend only a fraction of His grand design. Time will unfold His plan as He deems fit. He treasures each and every one of His precious servants and Is Mighty in bringing His Plan to fruition,"

"Can He use me in His plans, father?"

"Of course, my son. If we offer ourselves as vessels for His will, He Will make us a vessel to accomplish His Plans,"

"How do I offer myself to be His vessel?"

"Pray, my son, tell Him everything you feel, pour out your heart to Him. He Hears, and He Listens to every word,"

"Awesome! I love Him, I trust God just like I trust you, father,"

"May your trust in Him shield you from the trials of this world, my son. He alone is worthy of our trust,"

His confirmation was a heartfelt melody to my ears, yet his dream hinted at the challenges he must overcome in his journey to fulfill a sacred mission.

I held fast to the belief that God's divine plan would unfold as ordained. For it is He who holds dominion over all things, elevating whom He pleases to the heights of wisdom in perfect timing.

Chapter 46 The Request

As the summer afternoon heat began to subside, my mind remained entranced by a dream from a few nights prior. Watching Pawkzawd and Nimaw play from my comfortable favorite spot on the veranda, I skipped through the pages of ancient scripture on dreams. Pawkzawd, nearing the age of ten, was patiently teaching his little brother the intricacies of one of his favorite games.

Meanwhile, my gaze wandered over a passage on the signs of approaching calamity as my thoughts remained in disarray, impeding my focus.

"Oh Lord, I seek refuge in You. I am not able to count my blessings. I ask You to keep them safe under Your divine presence. You alone comprehend the profound sorrow that has shadowed these innocent souls in the absence of their mother, as You have borne witness to the ache within my own heart from Negawr's absence. Her memory imbues my days with a joy beyond measure. I beseech You to safeguard her sons within Your eternal embrace.

As my attention returned to the scene before me, Pawkzawd was demonstrating to Nimaw the art of balancing a small stick upon two rocks. "Look closely, you must strike the midpoint right here," showing with his tiny hand.

Eager and enthralled, Nimaw awaited his turn, "Can I try? I can do it!"

Accepting the larger stick from Pawkzawd, Nimaw positioned himself eagerly and took a swing. The small stick soared through the air, landing a considerable distance away with a triumphant thud, further than Pawkzawd's previous attempt.

"Excellent shot, Nimaw! Where did you learn that?" The big brother praised.

Proud and joyful, Nimaw gazed up at his big brother, sharing laughter in celebration as they scampered off to retrieve the stick. Each echoing peal of mirth filled my heart with awe as I marveled at God's creation unfurling before my eyes. Their angelic laughter was the melody of the precious, simple blessings that grace our lives in this world.

As they returned with the stick, ready to play, I spotted my older sons entering the front yard from the distant gateway, walking together in unison.

"Hey, Pawkzawd, what are you up to?" one of them called out as they neared the children.

"Peace to you, my dear brothers. We are playing

with sticks. Would you care to join us for a game?" Pawkzawd said with a welcoming smile as he offered the stick to his biggest brother, Puyaw.

"Sure, but I'm not familiar with the game," Puyaw admitted.

"I can show you how. It is simple - we each have a marked small stick like this that we toss by striking it with this larger one. The one whose stick travels the farthest earns the first turn next time," Pawkzawd explained enthusiastically, happy to offer his big brothers something.

"Sounds like fun. Is this stick yours to lend me?" Puyaw asked.

"Yes, here, have fun," Pawkzawd offered with loving kindness.

For a moment, that rare and heartwarming scene filled me with a profound sense of joy. All twelve of my sons were gathered there as a team, conversing, playing, and cherishing each other's company.

Amidst this joyful sensation, a hint of unease crept in, prompting me to push it aside with conscious effort as the work of the devil. Whispering prayers, I immersed myself in the beauty of that moment and the blessings before me. The two young siblings radiated with happiness and excitement as they played with their ten big brothers.

"Praise be unto You, my Lord, thank you…"

"That was fun; you two go ahead and play while we visit father," said Puyaw as he returned the large stick back to Pawkzawd.

"Thanks, you can come and play again any time," Pawkzawd said as he gratefully accepted the stick.

"Okay, we will," the brothers said before leaving them.

Pawkzawd immediately called Nimaw, who had fewer chances to play, "Here, Nimaw, it is your turn." Nimaw brightened up, relieved to play with his younger brother, who was a better match and always thought of him first.

I had a strange feeling of a nearing threat as my sons walked up the stairs onto the veranda where I was sitting. Seeking The Lord's Grace, I turned towards them.

"Hello, father," they greeted.

"Peace and God's Blessings to you, my sons,"

"Do you want visitors?"

"Visitors are friends of God. Welcome, my sons,"

After the initial catch up, Puyaw suggested, "Pawkzawd and Nimaw are growing up so quickly, father. Have you considered letting them venture out to interact with other children? At least Pawkzawd can come along with us the next time we head out for sports or field work."

"I enjoyed watching you interact with them, my dear ones. They both admire their big brothers. You did not only make them happy, but I also enjoyed it. If you spend time with them here, I can enjoy it too."

Puyaw added, "I understand, father. Nimaw is still too young, but Pawkzawd should explore the fields more."

Others, too, had the same wish, as each took turns expressing it. "It is time for him to learn the ways of hunting," or "We can teach him to hunt, but learning the wilderness is part of that game," or "He needs firsthand experiences ..."

Among the ten, the youngest and most reserved, Asher, spoke with a rare burst of excitement and enthusiasm, "Why not tomorrow, father? We are planning a hunting trip. Please allow Pawkzawd to join us."

Although I was touched by their kindness, I could not shake off my unease with the idea. "Your offers are kind and generous, my dear ones, but the thought of Nimaw missing him weighs heavily on my heart. He will surely feel lost without him."

Their persistent persuasion was irritating me, but I did not want to be ungrateful for their affection towards their young brothers.

"My dear ones, he is still too young to endure the harsh desert heat. Perhaps when the weather cools down and he grows older, he can accompany you."

Pawkzawd and Nimaw came up the stairs together and settled beside me. Each rested a hand on my lap and listened carefully to our conversation.

"Please, father, allow him to go and explore the world with us."

"It really saddens me that you should take him away. I fear that the wolf should devour him while you are engrossed in play, and he is left unattended."

At the mention of the wolf, Pawkzawd and Nimaw tightened their grips on my legs, visibly unsettled.

Pawkzawd and Nimaw squeezed their grips on my legs. I looked at them and put my hands on their shoulders, silently assuring them of their safety.

"But father, if the wolf were to devour him while we are so large a party, then should we indeed first have perished ourselves,"

Another chimed in, "True, father, it is impossible for the wolf to get near him, let alone harm him with ten of us, strong and vigilant."

As a father, I strived to safeguard all my children. I felt drained and weary, but Pawkzawd's excitement grew at the prospect of playing with his big brothers, knowing they were ready to protect him from the wolf. Could my apprehension stem from my own conflicting thoughts despite my sons' apparent sincere intentions?

"Oh, father, would you please let me go with them? I will be safe with my big brothers," Pawkzawd pleaded with hopeful eyes.

A shiver ran down my spine as I locked eyes with his innocence, recalling his recent dream. I could not deny that Pawkzawd's brothers loved him and wished to spend time with him, much like many others, even strangers, did. Wrestling with paradoxical thoughts, I found myself torn between fear and faith in God's ultimate protection. As I hesitated to yield to their pleas, reluctance lingered strong.

"Well, my dear one, you may take your brother with you tomorrow. Puyaw, will you ensure

Pawkzawd's safe return?"

"Yes, of course, father, I promise!"

"May God protect you all. Do not forget God in your affairs. He shall bless you for your love and care for one another."

Drained of energy, a faint voice within me whispered in confused emotions, "Take back your words now," but it was too late. Their jubilant planning filled the air as they celebrated tomorrow's adventure. A sense of unease weighed heavily on my heart.

"Thank you, father. Pawkzawd will have a lot of fun,"

On their way out, each one of them padded Pawkzawd on the shoulder with uplifting words.

"Sleep well tonight, Pawkzawd," one whispered.

"Be ready to leave early in the morning," another advised.

Pawkzawd was beside himself. Feeling mature enough to join his older brothers' team.

"Thank you, father, I am so excited. I don't need to sleep tonight. It would be really cool if you could come along,"

"I will wait for you here, my son. Please take extra care of yourself, for both your sake and mine,"

"Yes, father, I will. I will miss you, but we will be back before dark,"

By night fall, my heart was consumed by serious turmoil. In the quiet night, I tip toed to check on Pawkzawd, careful not to wake him up as I prayed. I leaned in close, inhaling his sweet scent, caressed his little form from head to toe, and tucked the sheet around him before returning to my prayer spot.

He was not in his deep, usual sleep. On one occasion, as I leaned over, he reached out with his tiny arms wrapped around my neck,

"Why are you not sleeping, my son?" I inquired softly as we embraced.

"Come on, it's time to rest. You need your sleep to keep up with your brothers. Sweet dreams, my love,"

I wished for the night hours to linger long, but the hours slipped away fast.

"Lord, I wrap him up in prayers and entrust him to Your care. Please watch over him in Your Gracious Divine Presence …"

Chapter 47 Departure

The call of the rooster pierced the tranquil morning prayer while it was still dark, pulling me back to my earthly sanctuary of reflection. At that moment, Pawkzawd came running towards me. I opened my arms, welcoming his form that seemed to be enveloped in a soft glow as he nestled his sleepy head against my shoulder.

"Good morning, father, are they gone?"

"Peace and God's blessings to you, my precious one. The hour is near, but fear not, they will not leave without you,"

Relieved yet brimming with excitement, he pressed a kiss on my cheek before dashing off to get the bag we had packed together before he went to bed last night.

"I want to take a threat they love; what should I take, father?"

His and Nimaw's favorite snacks were always stored in a jar by the window.

"How about sharing your own snacks with them?"

His face lit up at the idea. "Oh, sure, but do you

think they would like them too?"

"I don't see why not. They are delicious, are they not?"

He reached for the jar and settled beside me, meticulously selecting one treat for each of his brothers as he named them with reverence.

"Take more if you want,"

Carefully placing them into his bag, he expressed his concern, "My bag is too small to fit more than one for each, father."

"Did you count one for yourself too?"

He paused for a moment, pondering my words. "Oh, I did not, maybe I should, to keep them company," he mused, a contented smile gracing his features as we shared a moment of laughter – a brief respite from the impending departure and the emotions that accompanied it.

As he slung the bag over his shoulder, its weight caused him to tilt to one side. I adjusted the strap by crossing it over his head to the other shoulder, ensuring a balanced distribution of weight.

"This should ease your burden, my son, you have a long day ahead,"

Taking a seat on the stone bench by the door, I watched him as he meticulously secured his bag, ensuring it was tightly closed. With a sense of satisfaction, he then stood before me as we embraced, our hearts heavy with a mix of emotions and the looming apprehension of separation.

"Is there no chance for you to come with us, father?"

"I am too old to catch up with you all in the desert, my dear one,"

"But you are not old. Next time, I want to go with you. Just the two of us,"

"How much fun would it be for you to run in slow motion?" I remarked as we laughed. "You should run fast, go, and have fun with your brothers today. But before you go, allow me to adorn you with this," I continued, pointing to the Redaw I was holding.

Setting his bag aside, we removed his shirt as I asked, "Do you remember this?"

His eyes widened in recognition, "Oh, yes, how could I forget, father? It is the one I learned a lesson about the thief at Aunt Farah's,"

"Yes, good memory,"

"Wow, it is so soft and beautiful,"

"This Redaw is anointed and blessed with hidden powers," I explained as I carefully wrapped him in it. "My father, Farshawd, passed it down to me as it was handed down to him by his father. Now, I entrust you to continue our sacred mission. Are you ready?"

"Yes, father, what am I supposed to do?" curiously he inquired with reverence.

"Remain the God-loving person that you are, and this, my dear, must stay as our secret,"

"Okay, father, our secret feels so soft and cool. I will be careful in keeping it clean,"

"Keep it on, my son, while you are away,"

"Yes, father. I will. Thank you. I am really excited to join my big brothers in their fun,"

We dressed him with his shirt back on over the Redaw. Once done, he held me tight as I combed his silky hair with my fingertips.

"Father, why are you crying?"

"Nothing serious, my dear one. I am thinking of how difficult it will be to wait for your return,"

"But, father, it is just one day,"

"Yes, my son, for the span of a lifetime can sometimes be as fleeting as a single day, or even less than a few hours of it,"

Nimaw had woken up dashing towards us, clutching Pawkzawd's hand as if to keep him from going. Soon, Nanny entered the room with two cups of milk. I handed a cup to each, hoping to divert Nimaw's attention.

"I bet you this milk is fresh from your favorite cow," I teased as their sweet melody of giggling laughter filled the room.

Sipping their milk with one hand still intertwined fingers, the older brother set his expectation from his little one, "Nimaw, I entrust you with caring for father in my absence. Tomorrow, we shall have fun together, shall we not?"

Nimaw nodded solemnly, embracing his newfound responsibility. Just then, Nanny returned with a mysterious bundle in her hand.

"I have your favorite lunch here, Sir. Pawkzawd," she announced as she handed the bundle to him with a loving smile.

"Thank you. Is there something for all my brothers, too?"

"Yes, dearest," she replied warmly as she deftly made room in his bulging bag.

Suddenly, all heads turned towards the beckoning call of "Pawkzawd!" as the silhouettes of my sons appeared in the distant corner of the yard.

Upon catching sight of his brothers approaching, Pawkzawd embraced me tightly, unable to loosen his grip. A shiver ran down my spine, with a peculiar sensation gripping my chest.

To dispel the emotional weight of the atmosphere, I pressed a tender kiss on his cheek and gently guided his gaze towards the steps, urging him to move forward. He wrapped Nimaw in a long, comforting embrace, then slung his bag around his neck as we had practiced and headed towards the steps.

His brothers lingered below in the garden for him to join them, "Goodbye, father," their tone laced with an unexpected chill that struck me as peculiar. I realized that their farewell was unusually inconspicuous. Typically, they would come to seek my blessings before embarking on a journey, a gesture of reverence that was noticeably absent this time.

I lifted Nimaw into my arms on the veranda, and together, we watched Pawkzawd making his way down the stairs. Nimaw's tears streamed down his cheeks in quiet sobs as he clung to my neck tightly with both hands.

Just as the urge to scream and beckon him to stay consumed me, he retraced his steps, bounding back up the stairs. Kneeling to his height, I enveloped him in my embrace with my free arm. He swiftly kissed Nimaw's, then me on my hand holding Nimaw, before freeing himself from my arms and rushing back down the steps to catch up with his brothers.

"God be with you, my son," I called out, watching them with Nimaw as they walked away into the distance.

"Goodbye, Father, I will be back soon," his words echoed in the air.

"God be with you, my son," I repeated, my prayer a whispered plea for his safe journey.

Pawkzawd turned and waved as we mirrored his gesture until he merged with the waiting caravan, disappearing from our sight in a silent farewell.

The day proved to be a difficult one for Nimaw and me as we navigated through it without Pawkzawd by our side. Little did we know that our challenges would only grow harder with the relentless passage of time.

Chapter 48 The Wolf

Throughout the day, I toiled to divert Nimaw's attention from his yearning for Pawkzawd. His ache of loss mirrored my own, yet I bore my emotions in silence, resorting to prayer, engaging in playful activities with him, and aimless strolls to occupy his restless mind.

By nightfall, my sons had yet to return. A palpable sense of anticipation thickened the air as we lingered on the veranda. With ssstrained eyes on stretched necks, we searched into the distance for a glimpse of their imminent arrival. Balancing on tiptoe to scan the horizon constantly, every fiber of my being attuned to any sign of their approach. Overcome by weariness, Nimaw succumbed to sleep in my arms. His faithful guardian and my loyal companion, Farah, tenderly carried him to his bed.

The late, moonless night wrapped us in a shroud of profound darkness. Even the stars appeared more distant and elusive than ever before.

As the clock neared midnight, ominous shadows crept closer in the distance, prompting me to dash down the stairs and across the yard. A chorus of anguished cries pierced the night air, setting my heart pounding with dread. Frantically, I scanned the surroundings for any sign of Pawkzawd, but he was nowhere to be seen.

"Where is Pawkzawd?" I implored each of them in turn in desperation, yet their tearless sobs offered no solace.

"Where is Pawkzawd? Speak to me," I pressed on in anguish.

At last, their stony silence gave way to hesitant whispers.

"Oh, father, we went to play; the wolf devoured Pawkzawd," one confessed, his voice quivering with fear.

"The wolf? And yet you stand here in one piece?" I countered in disbelief, seeking the truth.

" If our words fail you, behold his shirt; this stain is from his blood, a silent testament to the truth," another murmured, offering Pawkzawd's bloodied garment as a macabre token of their harrowing tale.

"You have invented a lie that will pass with you. This blood does not belong to Pawkzawd," as I held the fake blood stain in front of them, "I beseech you, just tell me the truth. What have you done with Pawkzawd?" I pleaded in desperation as they persisted in tearful confessions.

"Father, believe us, the wolf devoured him while we were at play,"

"You know well that is not true. I am asking you only to tell me the truth," I insisted.

Alas! Their eyes remained blind to the glaring inconsistencies in their fabricated tale as I looked at Pawkzawd's shirt that remained intact while supposedly the wolf devoured him. They were blind to the nuances of human blood versus other substances.

Their tears were akin to the crocodile's nature, and their honeyed words failed to sway me; I saw beyond their fake facade with unyielding clarity.

"I no longer recognize you. What have you transformed into, my children? Leave me to grapple with this anguish. Return with Pawkzawd in tow or tell me the truth of what you have done with him," as I fell in tears of sorrow and anguish.

With each labored breath, my heart shattered into fragments only to painfully knit itself back together before being torn asunder again. In fervent prayers of lamentation, I beseeched God for patience and divine intervention, each inhalation a silent plea for Pawkzawd's safe return. Meanwhile, Nimaw slept undisturbed, unaware of the turmoil that beset our household.

At the break of dawn, Nimaw woke up and made a beeline for Pawkzawd's vacant bed to face confusion. Concerned, he scampered over to me.

"Father, Father, Pawkzawd is not in bed," he exclaimed with fear and curiosity.

"Yes, my dear, he has not returned yet."

"Why? Did they sleep in the desert?"

"No, my precious one,"

. "Did the wolf devour him?" he inquired; his eyes widened with apprehension.

"No, my son," I whispered. I cannot say with certainty where he is, but we must have faith and patience. Trust that God will guide us and reunite him with us, safe in our arms," I murmured from my aching heart to soothe his troubled soul as well as mine.

"When, father?" he pressed, searching in my eyes for answers.

His disappointment poured forth in an unending cascade of questions, each one a dagger piercing the fragile veil of composure I struggled to uphold. Despite my best efforts to project tranquility for his sake, he discerned the underlying anguish stirring within me.

Seeking solace, he wrapped his small arms around my neck, resting his head on my shoulder, he wept in silence. His quiet sobs resonated within the hollow of my chest, reflecting the depths of my own grief.

All day long, I sought to distract Nimaw from the ache of missing his brother. We felt adrift without him, having never been apart before. In my heart, I prayed, struggling to conceal my own agonizing anxiety for his sake as we wandered aimlessly, taking restless walks along the path where we hoped Pawkzawd might appear at any moment."

Afterword

In the revealed stories of the outstanding characters in
human civilization

lie instructions for those endued with knowledge

accessible only when one's will is surrendered

to The Divine Will

through conscious endeavor,

relentless pursuit of closeness, and

overcoming ignorance.

These stories are not invented tales but rather

affirmations of the past,

serving as a comprehensive elucidation,

an exposition of a roadmap, and

an exhibition of mercy for those who embrace faith.

I hope that you have enjoyed

your journey with this book,

offering timeless wisdom to ponder,

particularly in times of uncertainty.

Please keep an eye out for the upcoming release of

Guiding Love, Book III

If you have any questions

or wish to share your thoughts,

please feel free to visit my website at:

pathofnoor.net

May the Guiding Love be with you

on your journey as you ascend towards

unlocking your fullest potential.

www.ingramcontent.com/pod-product-compliance
Lightning Source LLC
Chambersburg PA
CBHW071407090426
42737CB00011B/1385